KU-485-120

PSI POLICY STUDIES INSTITUTE

EUROPEAN CENTRE FOR POLITICAL STUDIES

THE PUBLIC IMAGE OF THE EUROPEAN PARLIAMENT

Edited by ANN ROBINSON

With CAROLINE BRAY

STUDIES IN EUROPEAN POLITICS 10

NOTTINGHAM UNIVERSITY LIBRARY

TELEPEN
6 00 310659 X

Policy Studies Institute 1986
All rights are reserved. No part of this publication
may be reproduced, stored in a retrieval system, or
transmitted, in any form or by any means electronic,
electrical, chemical, mechanical, optical,
photocopying, recording or otherwise, without the
prior permission of the copyright owner.

PSI Own Series Reports

Sales Representation: Frances Pinter(Publishers)Ltd.
                          25 Floral Street
                          London WC2E 9DS

Orders to: Marston Book Services
                          P.O.Box 87
                          Oxford OX4 1LB

ISBN 0-85374-357-6

Published by Policy Studies Institute
100 Park Village East, London NW1 3SR
Printed by Bourne Offset Ltd.

CONTENTS

Foreword

Dr. Roger Morgan, Head of the European Centre for Political Studies, Policy Studies Institute

The European Parliament has suffered from having on the whole a bad press, or at times no press at all. Even the election campaigns for Parliament are not regarded as very newsworthy, and most of its work gets little or no media coverage.

To explore the reasons for this situation, its implications and some possible remedies, the European Centre for Political Studies, together with the Parliament's London office, invited a group of journalists and other media practitioners, MEPs and academic observers, for a weekend of discussion at Wiston House in Sussex. The programme was coordinated by Dr. Ann Robinson, Senior Visiting Fellow at ECPS/PSI, who is to be congratulated on producing (with the able assistance of Caroline Bray) the present report.

As the record of the discussion shows, the weekend produced a lively exchange of (often opposing) opinions, and indicated a number of steps which both the media commentators and the Parliament itself might usefully take.

This report conveys, in direct speech, a very clear impression of the discussions at Wiston House. It was understood that the proceedings would be 'on the record', and all participants have been given the opportunity to clear their remarks for publication. Thus it goes without saying that responsibility for any statement recorded here lies solely with the individual contributor concerned.

Our thanks are due to the wide range of participants for their valuable contributions; to the Wiston House staff; to Gloria Hyatt for typing the report; and above all to Roger Broad, who has directed the London office of the Parliament for several distinguished years.

March 1986   310659   Roger Morgan

ii

LIST OF PARTICIPANTS

Caroline Bray, Policy Studies Institute

Roger Broad, European Parliament London Office

Wendy Buckley, SDP

David Butler, Nuffield College, Oxford

Ivor Crewe, University of Essex

Brendan Donnelly, European Democratic Group, European Parliament

John Eidinow, BBC

Pamela Entwistle, Kangaroo Group

Adam Fergusson, Political Adviser, FCO

John Frears, Loughborough University

Win Griffiths, MEP - Vice-President, European Parliament

Mrs. Griffiths

Nigel Hawkes, The Observer

Stanley Henig, Preston Polytechnic

Paul Hodgson, Former Head of French Service, BBC

Terry Lancaster, Former Political Editor, Daily Mirror

Alex MacLeod, The Scotsman and BBC

Paul McKee, ITN

Roger Morgan, European Centre for Political Studies

Roy Pryce, Federal Trust

Ann Robinson, University College, Cardiff

Colin Seymour-Ure, University of Kent

Richard Simmonds, MEP

Carole Tongue, MEP

Norman Webb, Managing Director, Gallup Poll

David Wilkinson, Hatfield Polytechnic

Jean Williams, Polytechnic of Wales

SESSION ONE: INTRODUCTION

Ann Robinson, Lecturer in Politics, University College Cardiff and Senior Visiting Fellow, Policy Studies Institute

In order to understand why we are gathered together this weekend at Wiston House to consider the public image of the European Parliament we need to look back to the discussions that took place last October when a similar group of people gathered together here to consider the role of the European Parliament in the European Community policy-making process. The first conference was focussed on the institutions of the European Community and the interactions between them. It was, perhaps, somewhat inward-looking and some of the participants drew attention to this feature of the talks and discussions. From time to time during that weekend participants referred to what they considered to be the poor public image of the European Community in general and of the European Parliament in particular. As we came to survey and assess all that was said during that weekend and to write it down for publication a clear sub-theme to the conference emerged. Over and over again the participants were drawing attention to the poor public image of the Parliament. Clearly, this was a theme that merited separate consideration.

Overall, at the last conference, the general impression was that the European Community as a whole suffers from a poor public image but that the European Parliament, as it is a directly elected body and supposed therefore to represent popular opinion within the Community, must do all it can to appeal to the general public. If it, apart from other Community institutions, has a poor public image, then that is a serious matter for its legitimacy. All those who took part in the first two direct elections know how hard it is to sell the Parliament to the electorate. And those who have been elected as MEPs know that they have to work hard to make themselves visible to the electorate.

It is worth comparing the European Parliament with our own national Parliament. Has the British Parliament itself got a good public image? At one level it has not. We are all only too familiar with the "Ya, Boo" impression of the

1

House of Commons conveyed by the radio broadcasts of its proceedings. But, at a deeper level, it has quite a good public image. The MP is well-known and respected by his constituents, not least today because he is increasingly seen by them as a welfare officer, an institution of last resort for citizen's grievances against the state. Ordinary people do focus attention on the House of Commons and its members. The MPs are visible to the electors. The media, too, see the national Parliament as an endless source of copy, in particular as an endless source of gossip, for some MPs are on the way up to Government office, either in this Parliament or the next, and others are on the way out of favour. There is a long, long tradition of using Parliament as a means of advancement, at least since the times of the first Elizabeth. The House of Commons is one of the great public stages.

But, so far, ordinary people and the media have not focussed on the European Parliament in the same way. As we saw when we met here last October, interest and pressure groups have most certainly begun to turn their attention towards the European Parliament and its members, but these bodies are not the ordinary electors, nor do they necessarily represent their views.

This weekend, therefore, we are going to explore the image of the European Parliament as it is seen by the voters, and by the media who, as the word indicates, mediate between the voters and the Parliament, and we shall also look at how the Parliament is viewed by the parties, who along with the media act as intermediators with the task of organising and mobilising the voters to turn out at elections and vote.

If, in the course of our discussions, we are able to identify particular problems in the promotion of a good public image for the European Parliament then we may also, perhaps, be able to offer a few suggestions for the future. There can be no doubt that the future success of the European Community depends in part on the success of its only elected body, the Parliament, and that the success of the Parliament depends upon its good public image among the voters. The success of the European idea ultimately depends upon the goodwill of all the ordinary people of Europe and the great hope from a directly-elected European Parliament was that it would establish firm links between governors and governed in the European Community.

SESSION TWO: THE EUROPEAN ELECTIONS AS AN INDICATOR OF PUBLIC OPINION

Professor Ivor Crewe, University of Essex

In April 1962 Roy Jenkins persuaded a reluctant Gaitskell to meet Jean Monnet, the 'father of Europe'. Gaitskell relentlessly pressed Monnet over problems of British entry. Thinking the questions besides the point, Monnet protested 'You must have faith'. Gaitskell was unimpressed: 'I don't believe in faith. I believe in reason and you have not shown me any'. (Philip Williams, Hugh Gaitskell, p. 708)

Integrationists had faith in the first direct elections. They believed it would produce a 'great leap forward' in the legitimacy of the European Community. They assumed that MEPs would demand and obtain more powers for the European Parliament, which would in turn invest it with even greater legitimacy.

The integrationists' 'ideal' for direct European elections had five basic components:

(1) Common issues would dominate the European election campaign (i.e. issues about the structure, development and role of the Community or issues that were common to the individual member states which for their resolution demanded a Europe-wide solution).

(2) The campaign would be fought by transnational European Party organisations, not by national ones.

(3) The status accorded to the European elections by national politicians would be equal to or greater than that given to national elections.

(4) The result of the election would be interpreted as the European electorate's verdict on the European Parliament's record on European issues and a 'European Swingometer' could be applied in interpreting the results.

(5) The European election would generate media coverage, and this would encourage a high turnout of voters.

As criteria for genuine european elections these are very exacting, but they can be used as a benchmark to judge the actual elections. In both 1979 and 1984 reality fell far short of the ideal.

In the first place there is the question of the emergence of European issues. Events that took place in the preceding year certainly gave the opportunity to campaign on European issues. There were four main issues:

(1) Enlargement with Spain and Portugal;
(2) the budget crisis and the Common Agricultural Policy;
(3) the Spinelli initiative for reform of the Community institutions; and
(4) the specific British budget problem.

Action on these issues was not confined to the Commission and the Council: the Parliament also dealt with them. In some cases the Parliament's action was quite dramatic e.g. the vote on Spain's entry and the veto on the budget rebate for Britain. These issues had also been the subject of crisis 'summits' in Stuttgart, Athens, and Brussels, which had resulted in a considerable extra amount of coverage in the press.

Then there were issues which clearly had a European dimension such as the recession, unemployment, the environment, and energy, and a means of campaigning on European issues certainly existed: three important transnational party groups, consisting of the Liberals, Socialists and Christian Democrats, had been established.

Yet, in the event, in each country the key issues in the election were not European but centred on the domestic record of the national Government. These domestic issues, which were of little relevance to the European Parliament, varied from country to country. In the Netherlands Cruise Missiles, in France crime and immigration, and in the United Kingdom unemployment and the abolition of the Greater London Council. This last issue had more influence on the size of the swings in the election than did any other issue in the UK.

The only country to concentrate on European issues was Denmark, where the negative question of continued membership of the Community was paramount.

Politicians encouraged the concentration on national issues. In the UK Mr. Kinnock saw the campaign as providing an opportunity to knock Mrs. Thatcher at every press conference and he was obviously advised by the opinion polls to concentrate on national issues.

The second criterion, transnational party organisations, suffered from a number of limitations. Some European party groups such as the neo-Fascists and Communists have no extra-parliamentary organisations and other European party groups have members in only one or two of the Community countries, such as the European Democratic group which is primarily composed of British MEPs. The Socialists, Liberals and Christian Democrats are the only real transnational European party groups, and of these only the Liberals had a transnational campaign strategy. The Socialists tried to establish a common manifesto and common campaign but failed to do so because some Socialist parties (especially from the newer member states such as the UK) remain divided from their colleagues because they are hostile to further integration of the Community.

There are other features of the relative failure of the transnational party organisations. The bulk of the money raised by the Community for the elections was distributed to national parties, not used by transnational European party groups. The Socialist Group, for example, retained 15 per cent for itself, giving 22 per cent to the Confederation of Socialist Parties and the remaining two-thirds to each member country's Socialist parties. The Liberals gave three-quarters of their election money to the national parties, and the Christian Democrats passed the major part of the money they received to the national parties. The organisation and supervision of the campaigns therefore remained in the hands of national parties. In the UK the Conservative Party took over the campaign, to the chagrin of the Conservative MEPs, and the transnational parties just melted away during the campaign.

The third criterion, status of the elections in the eyes of politicians, also fell short. The European elections were certainly seen by politicians in most countries as 'second rank' elections and the leadership did not campaign hard. In the UK neither Thatcher nor Kinnock ranked the elections as particularly important, if one compares the daily press conferences by Thatcher and the twice-daily conferences by Kinnock during the general election with Mrs.

Thatcher's total of four during the whole European campaign. Mr. Kinnock did slightly better, but he did not hold daily press conferences.

A similar attitude was displayed by the Alliance. Neither Shirley Williams nor Bill Rodgers were willing to stand as European Parliament candidates, and they are supposed to be pro-Europeans. Only three former SDP MPs contested seats in the European Parliament.

The effort to end the dual mandate for British MEPs reveals where politicians' true preferences lie. Of four Conservatives holding dual mandates in 1979, three resigned their European seat in 1984 and only one, Tom Normanton, resisted the pressure to give it up. Only James Scott-Hopkins (who was at the time leader of the group) kept his European seat. No Westminister MP resigned in order to fight a European seat, although some who had been defeated in the 1983 general election stood.

Seven of the 1979 intake of MEPs (eight including Ann Clwyd) successfully stood as Westminster candidates at the 1983 general election. None of the five new MEPs who were formerly Westminster MPs had actually resigned their Westminster seat to stand for the European Parliament. Of these five Bob Cryer has already been offered a safe Westminister seat; Les Huckfield has made it clear that he is looking for one; and Joyce Quin, elected to the European Parliament in 1979, has been adopted for Gateshead East. The European Parliament is regarded as a stepping stone to Westminster (rather like the Chairmanship of a County Council) or a step down if MPs slip.

The behaviour of leading members of other national parliaments displays the same set of priorities. The Times Guide to the European Parliament pointed out that 79 of those elected as MEPs were already distinguished politicians (Tindemans and de Clerq from Belgium, Mauroy, Cresson, Chirac, Marchais and Messmer from France, Brandt and Bangemann from West Germany), but that none actually played an active role in the European Parliament. They had simply allowed their names to appear at the head of their party list to mobilise the vote.

The fourth criterion, interpreting the result as a mandate, falls short too. There is no real sense of the European vote indicating preferences on European issues or on the organisation of the community. The campaign was not presented as an opportunity for the electorates to vote in terms of West European politics and policies. The party groups were not organised so as to offer similar choices to electors in all the European states. (See Michael Steed, 'Failure or long haul: European Elections and European Integration', Electoral Studies, vol. 3, no. 3, December 1984, pp. 225-234). The parties took no position on European institutions except before the Spinelli initiative, and the politicians did not encourage voters to vote on European issues.

In Britain:

40 per cent claimed to vote on national issues
19 per cent claimed to vote on European issues
32 per cent claimed to vote on both

and the figure of 19 per cent claiming to vote on European issues would appear to be an exaggeration.

There was no broad movement of votes to the left or the right across Europe. France and Greece moved to the right and in Italy and in the UK the move was to the left. The result was no change in the political composition of the European Parliament as a whole. But there was possibly a change in the balance between federalists and nationalists as the nationalists did better in 1984 than in 1979 (British Labour, French National Front, Greens in Germany and MSI in Italy). But the reasons that these people were elected owed little to their anti-federalist position: it was more a protest vote on domestic issues.

The German political scientist Karl-Heinz Reif has described the European elections as 'second-order elections'. In all countries the turnout was lower than at general elections, they were used as an opportunity to give a verdict on national governments, and they provided an opportunity for radical or extremist parties to be elected because the outcome was not the election of a government. In every member-state (Denmark excluded) the European elections were like local elections where the elector could say 'Ya-Boo' to the party in office at home. They are used as a referendum on the incumbent government. So the MEPs' fates were determined by national party leaders and not by their own efforts.

The final criterion for judging the European elections is turnout, which might be regarded as a measure of public attitudes. In the EC as a whole there was a small drop in turnout, from 61 per cent in 1979 to 57 per cent in 1984. By general election standards this was low but it was not 'catastrophic'. Turnout is lower in US presidential elections and in democratic Switzerland. But the reduction in turnout must be a disappointment for those who foresaw a legitimising role for the new Parliament.

Michael Steed has pointed out that the real drop in turnout between 1979 and 1984 was probably higher than 3 per cent, that is if one excludes from consideration those countries with compulsory voting (Luxembourg, Italy and Greece), or where there were special factors in 1984 or in 1979 (Britain, Denmark and Eire). The three remaining countries, France, Germany and the Netherlands, where there is voluntary voting, were all founding members with favourable attitudes to the EC and were holding, in effect, mid-term elections. The actual drop in turnout was 7 per cent, to 55 per cent. So the true turnout drop is greater than might appear.

The UK in particular wins the European elections apathy award with a turnout of 32 per cent, the same as in 1979. This figure is well below the turnout for local elections, half the turnout for the European referendum and half that for general elections. In the case of the 1979 European Election it came just four weeks after a general election. There was thus little campaign effort, particularly by Labour, the electors were 'roused to a fever pitch of apathy', and the turnout might have been better had the European Election not followed so closely on the heels of a general election. Thus in 1984 the turnout could represent a real drop rather than no change. The gap between the turnout in the general elections of 1979 and 1983 and in the two European elections widened in 1984.

Why was the turnout so low in the UK in 1984? The answer was obviously not the weather, for it was a sunny day with a light, long evening. Nor was it lack of resources for campaigning. The £4m for the two main parties was more than they had for the general election. Unlike a general election, or even local elections, less is at stake in a European election. The ruling coalition is not determined by the vote and the British electorate alone has no effect on the result. The European Parliament has few powers and has little visible effect on people's lives. These are the structural explanations for the lack of interest in European elections. But if these are the reasons to explain the low

turnout in the UK, why are they not equally perceived by
voters in all EC countries? Another problem with this explanation is that for it to be valid one would expect to
find the differences of view reflected in opinion polls
showing low levels of support for the European Parliament
and particularly low levels in the UK. Inconveniently, for
this explanation, the opinion poll data does not bear it
out. Asked to say how much effect the local Council,
central Government and the European Parliament have on ordinary people 70 per cent said that central government would
have some effect; 67 per cent said that local government
would have some effect and 59 per cent said that the
European Parliament would have some effect. The figure of
59 per cent was almost twice the proportion voting for the
European elections.

There must, therefore, be some other explanation for
the low turnout. Was it perhaps the quality of the
campaign, the visibility of the campaign? Four weeks before
the election only 13 per cent of those polled knew that the
election was coming (but 55 per cent were in favour of an
election being held), only 7 per cent knew the name of their
MEP, and only 15 per cent had noticed publicity about the
Parliament.

Why did all the 55 per cent who thought European elections a good idea not vote? Is it possible that the British
are more hostile to the European Community than other
nations? Certainly the antis sat on their hands during the
campaign. But this only explains part of the low turnout.
There is slightly less enthusiasm for the EC in the UK than
in other countries but the differences are slender and do
not explain why the turnout is lower in the UK. An opinion
poll taken in October 1983 showed that the proportion of
people who had seen or heard something about the European
Parliament recently was 48 per cent in the EC as a whole and
48 per cent also in the UK. On other questions, too, the
British held attitudes that were not so very different from
those in the EC as a whole, though bigger differences emerge
on the question of whether the Parliament should play a more
important role (EC 59 per cent in favour, British 48 per
cent) or should have more power (EC 67 per cent, British 59
per cent). These are but small differences and are not
enough to explain the lower turnout in Britain.

We now come to the question of whether the anti-
Europeans turn out less. There is no evidence that in

9

Britain the anti-Europeans turn out in substantially lower proportions than pro-Europeans, or that Labour supporters (anti-European for the most part) were less likely to turn out in 1984 although this had been the case in 1979. On the contrary they were somewhat more determined to vote in 1984.

The explanation for the low turnout must be sought elsewhere than in popular attitudes to the European Parliament or the Community. Elite attitudes towards the elections and the Community influence turnout at the election. Elite attitudes are revealed by the amount of attention paid to the election by the media. There is little hard evidence that the UK media paid less attention to the election than the media in other EC countries. But the amount of knowledge of the Parliament before the election campaign began was much lower in Britain than in other countries. This significant pre-campaign effect is a reflection of media attitudes to the European Parliament generally, and indeed, the campaigns in other countries were not much more effective than in the UK.

The low turnout in the UK may simply be due to the electoral system employed here. In Northern Ireland where they used proportional representation the turnout was much higher (64 per cent). In the Republic of Ireland proportional representation was used in both national and European elections. Turnout in their last general election was very similar to that in Britain. The general attitudes towards the EC are similar there to those found in Britain. Yet at the European election the Irish vote was 48 per cent in 1984, as compared with Britain's 32 per cent. That provides a better comparison than Northern Ireland because in Northern Ireland the leading personalities stood (Paisley, Taylor, Hume) and this could have had the effect of increasing turnout. No such leading personalities stood for election to the European Parliament in Britain. There may be some scepticism about the effect of the electoral system however. The Eurobarometer asks a question about tactical voting and there was no more tactical voting in the UK than elsewhere. It is about the average for the EC. The lack of PR in Britain may have an indirect effect. Proportional representation in other countries induces a different electoral culture. Electors expect the result to produce coalitions and do not expect a clear winner or loser. But the British are not used to elections that produce no decisive outcome. They see elections as cup finals between competing teams. They do not, therefore, take the European elections seriously.

We might also ask whether the low turnout reflects upon the legitimacy of the elected European Parliament. There is evidence that the very event of the election made the Parliament more visible to the electorate. In April 1984 the Eurobarometer asked whether the public had seen or heard anything about the European Parliament. 75 per cent replied that they had. But, by October 1984, this figure had fallen to 67 per cent. In the UK the proportion fell from 72 per cent to 58 per cent. The short burst of publicity occasioned by the election had a very short-term effect.

Only 7 per cent in the EC as a whole and 8 per cent in the UK regretted not voting. Guilt feelings about lack of participation were hard to come by, particularly in the UK where a sample of 84 per cent of those not voting reported that they had no regrets at all.

Jean Monnet's faith has not disappeared, but we should recognise that in some member-countries like Britain, the spirit of Gaitskell's original scepticism is stronger.

Discussion

The media are not usually cast as part of the elite. The media explanation for the low turnout is a convenient one but does not hold water. A survey held on the day of the election showed that a high 83 per cent said that they had seen something about the European election on television. But few people were called upon by a representative from any of the political parties. It was between 6 and 9 per cent for the European election as against 22 to 33 per cent for the general election. Certainly, there was little information about the European election in 1979. The fact is that the parties do not think that the European election is of great significance to them. And this view is reflected in the lack of turnout. All that the media do is to respond to a lack of party activity.

Parties might do a 100 per cent canvass for County Council elections and find 60 per cent of the people in. But contact was only made with 5 or 10 per cent of the electorate in the European election. And the reason for this was that people simply did not understand why we were knocking on their doors. There was no point in the European

11

election for them.

The election did not attract any particular new talent. The higher turnout in 1979 was due to that being the first direct election. In 1984 there was an all-pervading sense of unimportance. Both the major parties were at fault. The Labour Party Secretary, Jim Mortimer, actually went on holiday to Spain at the time of the campaign. And Conservative MEPs felt that Central Office did not take the election seriously.

On the other hand in one sense the elections represented a great stride forward. They were part of a new institution getting itself established. Although some may call these 'second order' elections, they were an extraordinary achievement and generally positive in effect. The European Parliament may attract as candidates those who are either on the way up or down politically, but it does at least attract them. Transnational parties are certainly feeble, but they do exist and hold common positions.

Wales increased its turnout. Why was that? It was not the campaign on the doorsteps. In one area where no leaflets were distributed the turnout was 32 per cent whereas in another where leaflets were distributed and where canvassing was carried out the turnout was only 25 per cent. In 1984 there was more activity by the Labour Party in Wales and there was the effect of the miners' strike. The media, too, gave relatively good coverage in Wales. The Thomson press had a Brussels correspondent. But the radio and TV in Wales did not let the candidates appear. Furthermore, there is the amount of money that flows from the EC into an area like Wales. While England received £3m Scotland and Wales got £7m.

We might question whether there should be more topics on TV about Europe. But, say the companies, people will not watch this sort of thing. We should also consider the question of a higher commitment to the cultural sense of belonging to Europe and pay more attention to learning languages. The election can be seen simply as political theatre and here one defect is apparent because one does not learn the result of the European election for days after it has taken place, yet a general election in the UK generates an excitement akin to that of Christmas.

A good turnout provides a better mandate: greater satisfaction and a feeling that members have been properly elected.

There is a big difference between national politics and the politics of the European Community. The voter knows what each national party's personality is: he knows what he is doing when he votes. He has a clear concept of the meaning of universal suffrage. But the European Parliament is a constructed thing like a film set. The parties in it are not recognisable and we are invited to vote for something for which we have never had to fight to get established. So it means little to us. Sensible people stay at home. Only mad people vote in European elections.

There was also a drop in turnout in Belgium. This was because the leading politicians paid little attention to their European duties. Even the Italians, who are known as good Europeans, deserted their European duties. For example, Malfatti left Brussels for a junior job in Italy. The same goes for the French socialists. They desert their European duties. This phenomenon is due to the fact that power has moved from the Commission and out to the states. Lip service is paid during the elections in press conferences by national politicians so that their party list will be elected to the Parliament but basically the national Governments do not want to surrender power to Europe. Then the procedure of the Parliament itself is not good for the media. We may have to wait three days for the results of a vote. And Strasbourg is no ideal place to report from. It is hard to get MEPs to speak on the BBC: They are certainly not queueing up. It is a question of power, and power in Europe has moved back to the nation states. See, for example, how the MEPs are treated by their own Parliaments. They are invisible. National politicians saw the European elections as national elections. And this creates a vicious circle. The media naturally reflect the lack of power. There are not enough good Europeans - people like Heath, Jenkins, Brown - and some have left the scene. The media were keen at one time but not now. The rot has set in and reporting Europe has become just a job. And this is not just in the UK. There is a disjunction between the old European rhetoric and facts that are discernable about the operation of the European Community. The rhetoric stems from the Monnet days, and who would believe it now, Europe lacks supranationality. During the elections we tried to put on an all-night programme to hook up across Europe but it proved impossible so we wound up discussing national issues.

There are many reasons why the European Parliament is different from a national Parliament. MPs have ministerial batons in their knapsacks, but there is no parallel in Europe. The European manifestos are rather like those of the UK parties at the beginning of this century. The idea of a national party manifesto is a relatively recent phenomenon. The issue that the member governments now face is the weakness of the Community's institutional structure and the relationship of the national governments themselves in the Council of Ministers.

Finally, we have to ask what it was about the UK that made the turnout low. If you can answer that question you can answer another series of questions. The canvassers in the UK are not shyer than those in other European countries. Knocking on doors does not make any difference to turnout. The UK has not had the experience of struggling to ensure that we have a democratic vote in the European Parliament, nor had it to struggle for European integration itself as some other countries have. There is an intense meaning in the idea that the European Community brings freedom which is important in the minds of some continental people. Perhaps we should indeed look at the other end of the telescope and ask why 32 per cent of the British electorate were idiots enough to vote and why so few acted irrationally. Voting in any election is irrational for it is based upon a strong sense of party identification and exposure to a great deal of media information. Why did the turnout go up in South Wales? A lot of Labour Party supporters had a better reason to turn out in 1984 than they had in 1979. In 1979 Labour was demoralised. In 1984 there was a smaller variation in the turnout levels between the parties and Labour caught up because its loyalists turned out. Finally, turnout is related in some way to publicity. A significant comment made by many people was that the elections were a 'Eurobore'.

SESSION THREE: THE ROLE OF 'EUROBAROMETER'

Norman Webb, Gallup International, Secretary General of Gallup International Group (the European members of which carry out the Eurobarometer research - one for each country).

I conduct the UK end of Eurobarometer with Bob Wybrow. We meet with our French colleagues to discuss the questionnaire and the topics so that we can develop the English and French side by side and simultaneously so as to minimise cultural and language problems. The English and French questionnaires so developed then become the master copies from which the other countries develop theirs. The Danes and Germans mostly use the English version and the Italians and Greeks mostly the French as their base.

Since Spring 1974 the Eurobarometer studies have been carried out twice yearly (Eurobarometer itself predates this arrangement) taking a national sample of 1000 adults in face to face interviews. The sampling method used varies and is the best available for each country. There are 1000 respondents in each country except for Luxembourg which uses 300 and Northern Ireland (where the survey is carried out via the Republic of Ireland) which uses 400 as an addition to the 1000 respondents from the UK. All the surveys are done by Gallup affiliates except in Luxembourg.

The contents of the questionnaire cover basic trends, representing the hard core of regular questions, special topics that arise from time to time and work for other clients than the European Community itself. These include academics and research institutes but Eurobarometer is rarely used for commercial clients. Few commercial clients, in any case, see the European Community as a natural functional unit for their purposes.

Basic Trends

These include questions on the expectations for the coming year, the general situation, the financial situation of households, the fear of war and so on. We ask about the feelings of satisfaction with life and feelings of happiness, satisfaction with the functioning of democracy, and attitudes towards changes in society. (These are the sort of questions that were used by Ronald Inglehart, and I think that he's totally wrong in his view of Britain. We are not a 'post-industrial society' but a failed industrial society.) We also ask questions about the unification of Europe and the relative benefits to be gained from the European Community. These provide a judgement on membership. Then there are measures of the extent to which people consider themselves to be nationals or Community members and these are related to specific issues like the regions, the environment including acid rain, inflation, unemployment and energy needs. We also ask what people think about the speed of Community development. Is the idea of a United States of Europe credible? What we find as answers to these questions is that people do recognise the need for co-operation on matters like the environment but not on unemployment, where national measures are still preferred.

Special topics are introduced at the request of particular departments of the Commission. They include the attitudes of, and towards, new members; the roles of men and women in society, the developing role of women and the effect of unemployment on attitudes (this was done in 1975, 1978 and 1983 and reflects the activity of the women's liberation group in the Berlaymont); questions on European consumers - which showed hostile attitudes towards advertising; on scientific development, where we have asked whether people were for or against the European Community co-operating on scientific research. (Some replies on this were a bit naive). We have asked the peoples of Europe their attitudes to medical research. Then there was the big scare about computer banks. On the whole we have found attitudes hostile to defence research but positive to nuclear power. Other special topics have included retirement; children; energy; young people (in 1983); and the environment (in 1982).

The Role of Eurobarometer

There is an analogy beteen the European Parliament and a national Parliament which, like governments generally, would not carry out political surveys. We may query the legitimacy of studies carried out with public money (from the Commission) to determine political views. Eurobarometer may appear to violate the general principle that Governments should not carry out political surveys because it looks like a promotion effort for the European Community.

The Eurobarometer violates strict principles on taking a non-political stance because it is in a sense promotional for European concepts, but it is still the most democratic voice in the European Community. It is the only way that the voice of the people is heard. There have now been two elections, certainly, but in these the voice of the people was not shouting very loudly.

I have tried to persuade the British Foreign Office to conduct surveys on the attitudes of people in other nations towards the UK. This sort of market research is done by the USA, Germany and Japan as an important part of their foreign policy and their trade policy. But the Foreign Office claim that they are too broke and also they appear to have a profound distrust of opinion polls. I talked to them about this idea for twenty minutes and then the official said 'What is a survey?' It would be relevant for Britain to see how those countries most important to us see us. And it would also be useful for the EC to sound out attitudes in other countries outside the European Community such as the Scandinavian countries and Switzerland: how do they see the European Community, do they see it as a whole or still as the sum of its several parts?

There is some cultural bias in Eurobarometer. It is basically a French set-up with a Francophone thrust from the Commission in the topics they want discussed and in the framing of the questions. It is hard to stop Rabier from saying 'Europe' when he means the European Community, or to persuade him that it is not necessary in English to refer to 'le suffrage universel' when just 'elections' will do. Furthermore, a context is set through a whole body of questions directed towards the work of the Commission. Thus attitudes are softened. As a result attitudes in the UK appear more positive towards the European Community when measured by Eurobarometer than in Gallup's own polling.

In 1984 on efforts to unite Europe we found:

The Six	82 per cent in favour	
UK	69 per cent	" "
Greece	67 per cent	" "
Ireland	60 per cent	" "
Denmark	38 per cent	" "

British attitudes are getting more positive towards 'efforts to unite Europe' since 1973. They are more positive than those of Greece, Ireland and Denmark. But on the question of the benefits of membership the UK is the most pessimistic in 1984 of the ten member states.

	UK	EC
Yes	32	48
No	57	34
Don't Know	11	18

The UK shares with the Germans the feeling that we benefit less than do other countries.

On the question of whether membership is a good thing the UK is less keen than the average in the EC.

	UK	EC
Yes	38	58
Neither yes nor no	25	26
No	33	11
Don't Know	4	5

However, the majority would not like to see the European Community scrapped. The British are positive towards collective Community action in certain issue areas such as the regions, the environment, inflation, unemployment, the Third World and defence. But the UK is slow on unification, where together with Denmark, attitudes are moving against the idea of a 'United States of Europe'.

European Elections

Although awareness of the European Parliament's activities increased in the UK between 1979 and 1984 fewer British than other nationals were aware that there was an election approaching in April 1984.

	April 1979 per cent	April 1984 per cent
Aware of EC activity	25	72
Knew that a Euro election was pending	25	10
Did not know that a Euro election was pending	30	62

28 per cent of UK respondents and 33 per cent of EC respondents thought that the European election was important. On the reasons for not voting in the UK:

62 per cent did not know what the election was about
29 per cent thought the European Parliament had little power
21 per cent were not motivated by the campaign
12 per cent complained that national politics intervened
10 per cent thought that the European Community would not work

The 12 per cent who thought that there was an intrusion of national politics was a lower figure in the UK than elsewhere. But few (8 per cent) reported regret at not voting, while no less than 84 per cent of those who did not vote in the UK had no regrets at their failure to turn out for the European election in 1984.

Discussion

It proved possible in 1979 to estimate the likely European election results from the result of the general election that took place in the same year, but this was not possible in 1984. The polls reveal that most of the British people would really like the Community to go away, but this is a very different thing from wishing that Britain would come out while the Community continues. There is great volatility in attitudes so that in the UK we are building on shifting sands. In order to interpret the short-term variations in attitudes towards British membership of the Community it is necessary to know the precise date of the poll and the stimuli floating about in society at the time. No single finding can be treated with too much respect without knowing the circumstances. There have been several peaks and dips and the results are more like a roller-coaster on this than on any other single issue. Opinions about the Community are clearly not deeply rooted in the UK. Media headlines could have a big influence in the short term. One of the most positive readings of British opinions was at the time of De Gaulle's veto.

The Eurobarometer is one of the single largest research contracts in Europe, but it takes a long time to publish the results. The poll done in September 1984 did not arrive on the desks of journalists until June 1985. By that time it was an historical document and could not be used in the news context. The British can do polls quickly. Gallup is used to getting survey results out in a day but there are problems with Eurobarometer, particularly in clearing tapes and getting complex computer analysis. The UK section could, nevertheless, be ready in three weeks but other countries, such as the Italians, are slow in getting the material out of the field and into analysis. The policy is to collect the material together in one place, to do analysis in the Commission before publication, and translate into French and then into all the languages. This goes on in the mill of the Commission so all our fast work in the UK is wasted. The Commission which publishes Eurobarometer has no concept of deadlines or the idea of 'hold the front page!' for news.

When broad questions are asked some 70 per cent of the UK respondents are in favour of the general idea of European unity, but they do not link that concept specifically to the European Community and its particular institutions. Once specific questions are asked about the European Community and its institutions that goodwill vanishes. There is a distinction between the European Community and the general idea of European co-operation.

There are some worrying features about Eurobarometer. There are too many details on faulty skin-deep evidence of feeling. And it changes so much. It is recording changes in attitudes which are minimal and temporary, on matters on which people have not formed a clear opinion. There is a great reluctance among respondents to say 'Don't know' and attitudes are affected by party or leadership changes. Some of the questions, too, are vague. Of course, everyone is against pollution - there is an emotional response to such a question. Perhaps there is simply too much in Eurobarometer.

On the other hand there have been many relevant and detailed questions in the issue-based surveys like that on environmental pollution. The questions were relevant and precise enough and the replies made sense. But many of the questions are vague; they look good in classical French which influences the choice of concepts and of the varia- tions in the answer suggested ('strongly for', 'fairly for' and so on). Respondents actually get confused over these sort of responses. But sceptical views about these sort of questions are treated as disloyalty in the Berlaymont.

20

The timing of Eurobarometer is rigidly adhered to, polls take place in April and October each year. There is no clear message. The British people know there is an elected Parliament but it has no results that are relevant to them. The Parliament has not hit the headlines, certainly not much in the UK and things will get worse unless MEPs do their stuff.

People see a hiatus of power and information between the Parliament and other institutions of the Community. People seem to realise that the Parliament does not choose a Government. The surveys do provide some evidence of the people's awareness of the influence or lack of it of the European Parliament. There is some material comparing the European Parliament with national Parliaments, and the European Parliament comes off badly in the comparison. The questions on attitudes to the European Parliament and MEPs are asked after those on national Parliaments and national MPs so that the context is quite clear.

There must be some scepticism about Eurobarometer, which is paid for out of the Information Directorate-General's Budget. It is too global in its approach and needs to have more probing in depth. It is hopeless for the user. One problem is that it is difficult to distinguish elite from non-elite opinion. There is in the sample a sub-group of opinion leaders, distinguished through self-rating. This may be logically wrong, as a technique for defining elites. On the other hand it has been found to work. A question asks 'Do you lead discussion or influence others?' It is subjective but surprisingly sensitive to revealing elite attitudes and has been accepted as a measure. Perhaps some refinement of technique is required. Eurobarometer has never provided a measure of the intensity of feelings towards the European Community in the context of attitudes towards other issues and it is not clear where one would find more data on this. Questions on attitudes to the European Community itself and to European unity are set in a context and the amount of contextual detail is limited by the budget.

There are some problems of data collection. The big problem in Italy is the terrible inefficiency of their postal services which adds two weeks to the schedule and affects their own internal research as well. UK Gallup can do two surveys of 1000 respondents each week but the Italian company can only do twelve to every 100 that we can do. The

Greeks also are slow and very expensive, if all the islands are included in the sample. The Spaniards will also prove slow and the Portuguese, with their large rural community, expensive.

It is possible to understand why, before there was a directly elected European Parliament, the Commission undertook the task of surveying public opinion. But now that there is a Parliament with elected representatives surely their function is to be the link between citizen and institutions? Perhaps the Commission should no longer continue this work and should cease using a poll to push a certain kind of line on the Community. There is too much of a pro-European attitude in Eurobarometer.

In the UK it would be considered immoral for a government to do such surveys. Perhaps The Financial Times and The Economist should be commissioning public surveys and also the political parties, especially the Socialists and Christian Democrats, should be commissioning European-wide research for their own benefit. They could use surveys to target action and influences upon voters.

Eurobarometer is not used by the Commission in a constructive manner. The poor public perception of the European Parliament is found across the board from senior civil servants to the citizens. They do not know what the European Parliament is about and how it functions in relation to other European institutions. Even the party activists have not got a clue about the role of the Parliament. There are historical reasons for this. We have been members of the Community for less than a decade and there have been only two elections. There has been only a very short time in which to build up public awareness. And the European Parliament is not comparable to national Parliaments. There are limits to what can be done to overcome the difficulties. In some areas of the country, such as Wales, Scotland, and the North of England the MEPs are more fortunate for there are practical things they can refer to and this is reflected in the coverage given by the Press. There have been the grants and loans from the regional and social funds and the Coal and Steel Community and they get into the local press and the fact that the local MEP has played a practical role increases public awareness of the European Parliament. But Eurobarometer itself has not contributed to a greater public awareness of what the European Community is or what it should be or what the people think about it. If Eurobarometer was published more rapidly it might get more exposure in the media and then it might be used more effectively to build up awareness. The British Gallup can poll at a weekend, process on Tuesday and Wednesday and publish in the newspapers by Thursday. This means there is only a five-day gap between collection and distribution. The papers would be more likely to speak if they could get early publication of results.

It might be a good idea to abolish Eurobarometer. Someone could produce a general digest of polls, on the lines of the general digest already produced by Robert Worcester. The Eurobarometer exercise is unnecessarily ponderous. Even in research the best is sometimes the enemy of the good. Precise figures have less importance than broad figures and trends which are well backed by a range of material. A single person could do a bi-monthly summary of poll data. But the contrary view is that you simply could not get the same coverage for Europe by cannibalising and digesting because there is too little data from countries like Italy, Greece, Belgium or even France.

Eurobarometer material is not suitable for use by the political parties.   It is no use for explaining Europe to the electorate. A party needs staff to get it into a form so that it can be used for campaigning. There is lots of material coming from the Commission on the Regional Fund and the Social Fund but these funds only represent about 6 per cent of the Community's budget. What people are really interested in are subjects like the existence of huge grain mountains in Europe while people are starving in Africa. The European Parliament does better when it addresses that sort of problem of accountability and bureaucracy. It did all the things that it could on that issue to get the Commission to spend more money on food aid. But the answer to such questions lies not with the Parliament but with the Council of Ministers. And the food mountains do not belong to the European Community. They actually belong to the countries where they are located until they are sold to the Community. So giving them away to third countries would mean that member states would forgo payments due to them from the Community.

The problem of the Community's image lies with the national Governments and this is why the Parliament has a hard time establishing its credibility with the voters of Europe. The Parliament cannot force the Council of Ministers, but it can tell the media correspondents what is happening. It is helpful when newspapers have their own correspondents at the European institutions.

The trouble with Eurobarometer is that the information generated by it disappears into thin air. But it is not accurate to say that it has no use. It is used in some countries other than the UK. It would be a good idea if people were to write in to the organisation suggesting questions that should be included in future surveys. It would provide a different type of agenda setting for Eurobarometer and break the Commission monopoly. At present issues like grain and food aid are simply not getting in Eurobarometer because they raise questions that people in Brussels might not like to hear about.

Eurobarometer seems to stop short at the very point where it might prove to be interesting and relevant with information on issues that really concern people. It does not explore the reasons why people might feel disillusioned with the Community. These are the issues that are raised on doorsteps during election campaigns, but Eurobarometer does not tell us why the UK and France are disillusioned with the Community and its Parliament.

And issues on which people could feel gratitude to the Community are rarely promoted: for example gains by women under the Equal Pay legislation, consumer protection, and the environment. Everyday issues affect people and they identify with them; high-flown ideals do not attract them.

But it is difficult to promote these small everyday items in the media, however advantageous they might be to the European cause. The Community institutions should be doing research on what is needed to make the Community more interesting, exciting and salient to the electorate. We also need to know what the connection is between the European Parliament and the advances that have been made in the Community. For example, just what did it do on issues like sex discrimination and the legislation that had to be introduced in the UK to give effect to European directives? When, and at what point, did the Parliament achieve something in pressing for such advances? The Parliament, however, is in a difficult position because it does not really contribute so much on day to day questions of policy. But it must nevertheless take some share of the blame for the poor public image of the Community as a whole by missing issues which it could usefully cover.

SESSION FOUR: COVERAGE OF THE EUROPEAN PARLIAMENT BY THE BROADCASTING MEDIA AND THE PRESS

John Eidinow, Journalist
(who stressed that he was not speaking for or on behalf of
the BBC)

I will look at the present coverage of the European Parliament by broadcasting and develop a sketch of the outlets and what they provide. Then I will make some reflections on the nature of the coverage as seen by the broadcasters, and finally I will lay out some thoughts on the factors that are involved in presenting the European Parliament through the medium of broadcasting, using a rather arbitrary division into the intrinsic and extrinsic: the world of the broadcaster and the world of the Parliament. Finally I should like to consider whether there is a deeper-seated problem for the Parliament based on the fact that it has arrived at the table of history too late, at a time when its idea has passed by, and that this is what is reflected in its coverage. I do not want to originate a discussion on the role of broadcasters as mirrors or creators, nor on the language of reportage, but to consider the situation as it is.
    But first there is the question: if there is low public interest in and understanding of the European Parliament, is it because of the lack of broadcast coverage? Do the broadcasters carry some responsibility for this state of affairs? Eurobarometer showed that fewer European Community citizens knew or cared about the European Parliament in 1984 than before the first direct elections in 1979. Turnout in the election was low.
    On the other hand, if broadcasters take little interest in the European Parliament, is this not an accurate representation of a weak institution, not making the best of itself, reflected in an ambiguity of role, an institution that is actually very difficult to report within the constraints of the media? There are other questions that must be asked: what is to be the angle of reporting? Is the Parliament to be seen by the media as a sort of Westminster at a distance? Or is it a supra-national body reflecting a European perspective? It is not the role of broadcasters to represent hopes and aspirations. But equally, it is not a fair representation of the Parliament's work to concentrate on issues such as the renaming of Waterloo Station,

the cost of MEPs' travel and expenses and the amount of absentee voting that takes place. Nonetheless, positive publicity has to be earned.

I am in search of an adjective - what sort of broadcasting of the Parliament do we want? 'Decent', 'proper', 'extensive', 'routine'? These tell us very little. Should it be obligatory and if so of what? Should it be of the Chamber proceedings? I am not sure what the job is except to provide day to day broadcasting of news. Should there be a formal commitment as there is with Westminster or should we simply broadcast when there is 'news' or issue 'snippets'? The unconscious and misleading yardstick is perhaps the coverage of Westminster which is constantly present, and reached a peak of 34 hours of debate broadcast during the Falklands crisis. Regular use is made of excerpted material on the news and current affairs programmes nationally and locally, and Parliamentary actuality on other national and local radio and regional TV. Inside Parliament covers committee work and there is also Today in Parliament and Yesterday in Parliament. At another level there is routine comment on current Parliamentary and political issues by Government members and the Opposition. Then there are the appearances generally by MPs who are so easily accessible. If we have so much as a cat killed on a motorway the Chairman of a Select Committee will ring up.

I will now give a sketch of the present coverage of the European Parliament which, as you will see, is nothing like that available for Westminster.

Looking at the political outlets for regular coverage first on ITV: Channel 4 News has the occasional piece but no real European Community coverage, though what it does is expected to be in depth; A Week in Politics practically never covers European affairs or the work of the European Parliament, except for the European elections (A Week in Politics, is, however, under some pressure in the wings to cover the European Community more; but there is a feeling that much of it is very difficult to report on TV without boring the viewers); ITN made a whole-hearted attempt during the election period to cover the run-up to the election and election night. (There, too, there was a feeling that it was difficult to make the viewers feel that it mattered, that is except as a reflection on national issues between elections). There is no sense of any informal requirement to report or the feeling that, as a matter of routine, European Parliament proceedings should be covered. (There is no news value in the Parliament. And anyway the coverage of European matters through individual countries is not all that good - it is an uphill battle. People turn to the USA rather than to France or West Germany, because of cultural barriers. The media have a necessity to choose those items to which the viewer can relate. In the case of the European Community, and even more the Parliament, this is difficult both because they do not appear to matter and because the issues are very complex). Local ITV provides some coverage of the European Community on issues that are related to local interests such as fishing and farming. Anglia and Southern TV know for a fact that viewers will be interested in such issues.

The BBC (BBC TV News; Radio News; and Today; PM; The World at One; and the World Tonight) offers a big role to its correspondents in Brussels. There is also the Local Radio experiment; which is closer to the European ideal from the European point of view. In general, the BBC TV news tries to cover one story from each plenary session of the Parliament, if the news value proves worth it; this usually means only major events. That coverage is provided by the BBC's diplomatic staff, an important distinction. There is no routine coverage of the Parliament's work. The reason is simply cost. The Brussels correspondents cover news stories in Strasbourg and they also have the Council of Ministers and the Commission on their beat. Coverage of each is taken on merits and in the contest between the Parliament, Council and Commission, Parliament comes off as an inevitable bad third. It is, however, good for meeting people and for off-beat features and stories. Strasbourg is a useful place to get hold of people wandering about with not much to do.

The closest that we come to any routine coverage is the acceptance by the BBC of an informal requirement to cover the plenary sessions of the Parliament. This is done through The World Tonight aiming to place twenty minutes of stories by the end of the plenary week, using Westminster correspondents. But in the nature of things what The World Tonight does is not like Today or Yesterday in Parliament. A total of twenty minutes is not much to cover the Chamber itself and reports and features from around the Parliament. On the other hand The World Tonight has a slightly easier task, for it regards itself as an up-market programme which does not need to explain all references such as EMS, Green Money, and MCAs, for it assumes that the listeners understand these. And the programme has found the Parliament becoming a more interesting place with personalities like Leslie Huckfield and with the Greens. They detect, too, a

27

sense of Europe in the proceedings. But the cut and thrust of a national Parliament cannot be reproduced.

The variety of different types of reporter involved in covering the European Parliament - Diplomatic; Westminster; Foreign News Correspondent - must result in some unevenness of coverage. Westminster correspondents come from the close drama and gossip of Westminster to take on the complex affairs of the Community and its Parliament. A common criticism is that you have to be in Brussels to understand the EC and its institutions; to fly out for one week from Westminster does not supply that understanding. The foreign news correspondents are those best able to do the work of reporting the Community. They speak the languages and know what and who is important in other nationalities. The unevenness of coverage also represents genuine confusion as to what sort of news they are reporting. Is it home, foreign, diplomatic or what? This affects the nature of the coverage of issues that are complex and need depth.

So on to the BBC's local radio and English regional TV coverage. This is an important experiment. From September 1984 until September 1985 a 'dedicated' reporter has been working out of Brussels direct to 20 local radio stations and eight TV regions taking a similar service from Westminster as a model. They pick up local issues and get local MEPs to comment. National correspondents cannot provide a service in the sort of detail demanded by local outlets. The reporter lives in Brussels and is a direct link between the European Community and the regions and localities, by-passing Westminster and Whitehall. The reporters in the past have done more than respond to events in Brussels, they bring out news from the Community. This is not routine, obligatory, Parliamentary coverage on the national model but stories, interviews, features straight from Brussels or Strasbourg to the locality. Many stories are offered through this service on subjects like farming, regional policy, fishing, waste, textiles, police harrassment, nuclear waste, hothouse gas prices. Editors have been surprised at the enormous value of the experiment, there have been many stories, a high usage rate, and a tremendous sense of immediacy on items such as fishing stories after enlargement, steel and farm prices after the Council meetings. Here we have the example of a general reporter who includes Strasbourg on his beat as well as the Council and the Commission. It is important to have one reporter specialising in the European Community as a whole who can see the issues and the connections. It is an educative process for all. There is a great challenge for a man in this diffuse and less predictable situation than Westminster.

How do other broadcasters themselves feel about the European Parliament? My personal view is that once we hear the title 'The European Parliament' our eyes just glaze over.

To broadcast the Parliament is of limited news value, it is a peripheral institution and has no sense of power. It is boring and confusing. It lacks straightforward stories with good definition. It is hard to see what it does to spot issues and to see results. It is therefore inevitable that stories like those on proposals to rename Waterloo Station and the trips taken by MEPs to foreign places are highlighted. There are other questions. What sort of news is the Parliament - to be covered from what angle?

Should we be giving a European, supra-national perspective or context to the Parliament, if it means that all stories are from an altitude of 30,000 feet? My own direct experience, of European Election night, for example, is that all the focus is towards the impact on domestic politics.

Equally, it should be noted there is no great interest on the continent either, in Paris, Bonn or Rome. The Community is only of interest to them when it has an immediate news value. For any West European coverage, ITN is less well off than the BBC which does at least have correspondents in place in various countries in Europe who get to know the corridor politics, can cope with the language and understand the different cultures. But in Brussels there is a lot of 'Europe' to cover. There are the three major institutions of the Community plus NATO so Strasbourg gets a low order of importance. It is a Cinderella with no fairy godmother in sight. It is hard enough to sell Brussels anyway.

All the same, Britain does not do too badly by the Parliament, compared with other, seemingly more communautaire, countries. In 1983 Britain came third in the amount it transmitted from the European Parliament's audio-visual centre. Out of a cumulative total of 46 hours West Germany came top with 10 hours, Britain and Italy produced 7. (These are the amounts actually recorded, but not necessarily transmitted by, national TV). Luxembourg came bottom of the list and Ireland second from the bottom. It ought to be recorded that there is only praise for the co-operation of broadcasting staff at the Parliament, and the ready availability of people and facilities.

The major factor behind the broadcasters' negative approach is the element of cultural confusion. The European Parliament is nothing like our own dear Parliament with its defined parties, its debates, slanging matches, Whips and clear results. The European Parliament is constantly shifting, forming alliances and dealing with incomprehensible policies. Its practices, including the rapporteur system, are unfamiliar to us. And how do you define the green pound or the EMS in 30 seconds suitable for transmission to a mass audience? Then there is the language problem: interpreters are not fun to put on the air. There is also a substantial problem of cost. Broadcasting talks in a language of priorities. The costs are substantial to put in a reporter, crew and so on. And we have to ask whether we will get a news story out which will interest the viewers and the listeners. On such a scale of priorities the European Parliament does not rate highly. We will spend, however, on USA coverage where decisions are being taken in the White House and the Capitol that directly affect us on things such as NORAID, the strength of the dollar, MX Missiles and 'Star Wars'. In the area of the economy that is where it counts. And that is what the European Parliament is up against. Furthermore, the US is more accessible in terms of language and political culture.

All the foregoing are what might be termed the extrinsic factors which affect coverage of the European Parliament. Now we shall turn to the intrinsic factors. First of all there is the hybrid physical set-up which makes coverage more difficult. The Council meetings are in Brussels, the Parliament is in Strasbourg. It is not easy to generate coherent coverage through one pair of hands and achieve depth. There is lack of regularity of contact and there has to be much travel.

Then the procedure of the Parliament is not easy to follow. There are split votes, with another vote taking place two days after the first so there is no clear conclusion. The rapporteur system creates confusion and is not easy for the British reporter who is used to the Committee's Chairman taking charge of reports to the plenary session. The Council, the Commission and NATO are all easier in this respect. Sadly, there is the question of 'reportability'. Few of the MEPs are real professional politicians. A professional politician knows how to present an argument to the media in 20 seconds or 3 and a half minutes and how to angle remarks and how to top and tail. MEPs are not so adept. Few are real politicians, although there are some former Labour MPs trying to return to Westminster. There is a general predominance of academics, teachers, lawyers, writers and businessmen. In the UK delegation there is a predominance of people from business, academic, legal and farming backgrounds, in a delegation that scores below Strasbourg average for governmental experience. One quarter of the UK MEPs have no previous political experience at any level. They are of a lower average age, too. So there is a perceived lack of weight and skill. The foreign MEPs, apart from a few internationally known, are largely an unknown quantity to the home based British reporter or producer.

The nature of the Parliament itself poses problems. It makes an attempt to promote a European dimension in its organisational structure and on the issues that it considers. A reporter thus has to have some familiarity with international organisations. A Westminster reporter does not have that sort of experience. So, the European Parliament is not easy reporting for a culturally nationalist press and broadcasting system.

Another intrinsic problem is that of the nature of the topics. The Parliament has perhaps shown a tendency to concentrate in public too much on political affairs, though it has no powers or competence in that area of policy. It may be reaching for wider political issues which look as though they might prove popular but which lie in areas in which the Parliament's view is simply not important. It could look to the outsider that its concentration on these issues is just a waste of time. There is a disjunction between effort and impact. And who wants to report something that is a waste of time? One-third of the Parliament's activities between 1979 and 1983 were in areas outside its Treaty powers.

There is an essential lack of definition about the Parliament, about the comprehensibility of its work and its image. What are the real directions and the real thread of the European Parliament? Its lack of clear purpose and image does not make for easy broadcasting. It is not a parliament and it is not dealing with a government so it is hard to report.

At this point I should like to refer to Christopher Tugendhat's Montague Burton Lecture, in which he said that he would not, at this juncture, 'advocate any change in the

European Parliament's powers'. The Parliament

is still very much in the shaking-down phase of its
existence and trying to find a role. It has by no
means explored the limits of the potential influence
available to it under the present rules nor even begun
to establish itself in the public mind...In the mean-
time it is for the Parliament to prove itself, in
which case it will be able to increase its influence,
not for others to thrust powers prematurely upon it.
Its problem so far has not been lack of power, but the
inability to organise its business in a coherent
fashion and to mobilise a majority in support of a
consistent line of policy. The way in which it
shifts, sometimes almost monthly, from demanding
restraint on agricultural expenditure to calling for
even higher spending provides the classic illustration
of this.

This, then throws up a final question. Are we already
too late in calling for a European Parliament with a sense
of centrality and purpose? The current debate is on whether
it will develop a more central role in policy. If it does
not, the chances are that broadcasting coverage will get
less (coverage of the debates themselves would be too complex and detailed to merit consideration). To quote once
again from Tugendhat:

It is now clear that the hopes which were widespread
at the time of the Community's birth that the nation
state would wither away and die were misplaced.

Furthermore, we see in Europe the revival of local units as
the focus for political activity.

The faith, which was also prevalent at the time in
large, centralised units and the efficacy of
'planning' has also been destroyed by experience. The
idea that markets and competition are more likely to
lead to the greatest good of the greatest number is
enjoying a revival, and by no means only in countries
with ostensibly right of centre governments.
For these reasons the Community cannot be expected
to develop in a supranational fashion nor is it possible to conceive of a massive transfer of responsibilities from the national to the Community

institutions. Most people in most countries do not want to be run from Brussels. Moreover at a time when national governments themselves are trying to decentralise and to divest themselves of responsibilities it is absurd to advocate moving in the opposite direction at the European level.

If he is right, then this will affect the way in which the European Parliament is covered by the media in the future.

Terry Lancaster

Many of the general comments I was proposing to make have already been expressed by John so I shall not repeat them. I would only like to refer to another previous speaker, Stanley Henig, when he said he did more good by discussing the European elections in a pub than he did by door-to-door canvassing. I am sure he was right. We must admit that to the ordinary voters the elections were a massive turn-off. Fleet Street was well aware of this and covered the elections accordingly. As far as the general public was concerned the voters might well have been taking the advice given by the American comedian, Mort Sahl, when Eisenhower stood for re-election in 1956: 'Vote "no" on Tuesday - and keep the White House vacant for another four years'.

The brutal fact about the European Parliament was summed up in the Time magazine story about the Reagan visit to Strasbourg when it commented that the Parliament had 'less power than any other legislature in the Western World'. Fleet Street knows this and treats Strasbourg with about the same amount of respect as a British minor County Council. Newspapers, after all, invariably have too many stories for the amount of space available. Journalism is a matter of selection. The reaction of even the night editor of, say, The Times will be just to spike copy from Strasbourg with the comment: 'It's just not sexy'.

At one time, of course, The Times did try to cover Strasbourg. It gave space to Parliamentary reports from Strasbourg and gave its former Political Editor, David Wood, a regular European column. But all that ended as a result of two factors - lack of genuine news and rising costs. There was the same situation on the Daily Mirror, a popular paper but one which had been pro-European long before Britain's entry. I sent David Thompson, our Gallery man, to session after session but he rarely got his stories about the actual proceedings into the paper. After several nights of

33

frustration he would send something about 'Another MEP expenses ramp'. In fact, it might be argued that in view of the increasing trivialisation of the British press it is desirable not to have the Parliament covered because only unhelpful stories would be printed. Both The Times and the Daily Mirror have changed ownership since the days when Rees-Mogg and Cudlipp, both strong Europeans, were in charge. Now the deciding factor is cost-effectiveness and the cost per column-inch printed of having a man in Strasbourg cannot be justified.

Of course, if all the institutions were in Brussels a case could be made out for having a staff man there or even a well-paid stringer. But we all know that the chance of all the European institutions being based in one centre is out of the question in the immediate future. I predict that apart from specialist papers such as The Economist there will soon not be a single British staff reporter even in Brussels.

Fleet Street's apathy towards Strasbourg is equalled by the party leaders and the party machines. In the last European Parliamentary elections the parties almost ignored the European Parliament. They fought it almost entirely on British domestic issues. The best example was in London when the issue was not the European Parliament but the Greater London Council. Significantly London had the largest swing to Labour. With this in mind I imagine that next time the parties will concentrate even more on local issues.

The fact is that the two major parties mistrust Strasbourg and its MEPs. MEPs are hard to bring into party discipline. They are regarded as better off than Westminster MPs. All the original mistrust of Europe seems to come to the surface in regard to Strasbourg. Because there is no political will to increase the significance of Strasbourg the Parliament is deliberately played down in Westminster and Whitehall. And in turn it is played down by Fleet Street.

Of course it is not only Strasbourg which does not get proper coverage in our national papers. The Commons, though treated far better, still gets less coverage than at any point during our life-time. The so-called quality press, in addition to the popular press, is becoming more trivialised. Our political reporting compares badly with that in the United State and Europe. So the few stories which emerge from Strasbourg are also trivialised. I cannot believe, for instance, that the role of the European Parliament in the

34

British miners' strike was the most important story to come
from there in recent months. Yet that is what attracted the
notice of all our papers.

But there is life outside Fleet Street - as I found
when I left there. The European Parliament's London office
- and that of the Commission - pay quite a lot of attention
to our regional and local press. Provincial papers do not
have the same pressures on space. They are also anxious for
local stories. Of course there is less news coming from
Strasbourg than from Brussels but that should not hamper
MEPs. They should get associated with every European event
which affects their constituencies - new bridges, roads, social grants and so on. Whenever there is any event affecting
Europe they should be there - if possible with a
photographer. An Eisenhower Cabinet Minister named Charlie
Wilson, a former boss of General Motors, once got into
trouble because he said, 'What's good for General Motors is
good for America'. MEPs should adapt this saying: 'Anything
that's good for Europe is good for us'. They should concentrate on local papers - and local radio stations as well.
Local radio stations, particularly the BBC which concentrates on talk rather than pop music, afford wonderful
opportunities. My impression is that local papers have
greater reader penetration than national papers, because for
one thing they are round the house for longer.

The European Parliament has an information fund. How
is that used? Is it used mainly to ferry local party activists to Strasbourg? I get that impression. I may be
wrong. But what it must be used for primarily is to explain
and popularise the work of the Parliament. We have less
than four years to the next elections. We must do what we
can to make certain that they are not so dull as the last
ones. We must do what we can despite the knowledge that the
work of popularising the Parliament will never be an easy
job while there is no political will from the centre to help
the Parliament in any real way.

Discussion

A sharp distinction can be made between national and
regional reporting. On the whole British MEPs probably get
their money's worth from the media. But some reporters
still only see stories as being essentially pro or anti the
European Community. The Press all the time want MEPs to say
'Yes, it's good' or 'No, it's bad'. They encourage the sharp
quote. And the Labour Party is worse than anyone else at

35

conniving at this. Some MEPs feed on anti-European Community prejudice.

One solution would be to get the whole apparatus together in Brussels. When the Parliament last voted on the proposal to put all the institutions together in one place it had the second largest voting turnout in five years. About 100 members who appear as a rule only about twice in any year turned up to vote Yet the 200 working members of the Parliament would produce a majority in favour of a move to Brussels.

Another problem with reporting the actions of the European Parliament is that it is not the end of the line for any story, even if it does move to vote immediately after a debate has taken place. The discussion of the issue grinds on, perhaps for years, until the Council of Ministers takes the final decision on any proposal.

And there is much incoherence in the Parliament's stands on policy, as Christopher Tugendhat pointed out. There is often, as a result, no clear majority one side or the other. On European issues such as the future of the Budget and the Common Agricultural Policy, there are ideological splits even within party groups in the Parliament and then these are cut across by national splits. For example, in the Socialist group there is a majority for radical change in the Common Agricultural Policy, but it is narrow. This creates reporting difficulties.

The regional press is important to MEPs but local weekly papers can be frustrating to deal with for they show little pattern in their coverage of Europe and it is never possible to foresee what they will do. At times they will reject a strong local story; it all depends on what the other local stories are that week.

There may be a more optimistic view of the ultimate future of the European Parliament. There is some indication that it is edging towards the development of its existing powers as they stand now within the ambit of the Treaty. Parliament took the Council of Ministers to the European Court for its failure to develop a transport policy as outlined in the Treaty of Rome, and thus established that the Parliament can take the Council of Ministers to Court for failure to act. This may prove to be an important power in the future. But the Parliament has an uphill struggle.

Seeing that the Westminster MP has almost unrestricted access to the local press and clear rights in the constitution the MEPs think about moving towards the attractions of Westminster. On the other hand whenever local people are brought over to Strasbourg - those looking for funds from the Social or Regional Funds, for example - they are bowled over by the events that take place in the Strasbourg week, the number of meetings and the people that are about being seen.

Most of the weekly newspapers are still set in hot metal which is a slow process. The important thing for the MEP is to find out when they start setting, what is the paper's deadline and to get stories to them early.

The World Tonight has the only regular broadcast coverage of the European Parliament. But it is staffed by Westminster people. All the good Westminster stories come from the Chamber of one or other House. But if we look at the things that have been transmitted from Europe they were on subjects of interest beyond the confines of the Chamber including drug trafficking in Europe, terrorism, and women's rights. All of these went beyond the Parliament as strictly defined. And they depend for their success on the skill of the reporters handling them. Some Westminster reporters do not know how to cover such stories, some reporters do better than others, they have to be adaptable. But there is no rationality in the BBC at the moment about who is sent to report on Strasbourg. It's a lottery as to whether a story turns out to be really interesting, well done or not. On the other hand, it has to be said that much UK political broadcasting does go beyond the confines of the Westminster chamber and there is some analogy with European politics.

There is some inflation in the official figures of the amount of coverage of the European Parliament. A regional company will send out a team to cover their local MEP in the Parliament and this all gets added into the figures. So the figures given by John Eidinow do not show the actual amounts of broadcasting shown to the public. The figures do, however, indicate that in 1983 there was twice as much broadcasting as in 1982 after a long decline from a peak in 1979. Also there have been technical improvements which make coverage easier. At one time it was not possible to do live TV broadcasts from the Parliament.

Reporters covering the European Parliament tend to attack the institution itself. There is a lack of knowledge about the Parliament: it is not a legislature. If we were to remove the front bench from the Commons or the Lords they too would be in a similar situation. There would be little to report. If the European Commission take their seats then the Parliament is a legislature. It is hard for a journalist to focus on this constitutional reality. So it is wrong to say that the Parliament's time has passed. It is not yet come and it will develop if it can be seen as the place where the Government of Europe is made answerable for its actions.

On the other hand, it was argued that we should call the European Parliament an Assembly. There is a confusion of terms for the real Parliament of Europe is the Council of Ministers, and one should say so. We ought to be discussing the Commission as the Civil Service. There would be less of a feeling of disappointment if the terms were clearer. As it is people feel let down.

Some bias in reporting exists. At one time there were many top men in the BBC, and at the Foreign and Commonwealth Office who were pro-Europe. Edward Heath, when he was Prime Minister, got some action and set up a broadcasting office in Brussels. At one time The Mirror, The Times and others were pro-Europe. They are not so now. The national media are very powerful. The attempt to get a Euro-Radio consortium established was in the end torpedoed by the French, but it had no institutional support in the UK either, only from individuals. Even BBC 2, meant to be 'the best in the world', now shows snooker all the time. Why not put pressure on the BBC for more serious coverage of the European Parliament? There is one favourable indication: satellites should allow some room for European reporting.

In all the studies of news values and contents, the European Parliament becomes an 'ideal type' of the 'rotten subject' with a negative score on 'news values' as established by the media. This raises the question of how far the news media should feel obliged to cover the European Parliament. Ought one to expect more of TV and radio than of the press because of their obligations to 'inform, educate and entertain'?

The coverage of the European Parliament has two problems which are similar to those for science and religion. These are the question of the slot: what kind should it be and how big? and how far can you inject coverage into general interest programmes for the non-zealot? If the subject is a 'specialism' rather than suitable for a 'slot' as it is seen to be currently, then should it be on cable or satellite coverage? Regional media are picking up more in the way of specialised coverage than the national media and this might indicate that speciality outlets are the growth area for publicity about the European Parliament.

It may be that we are in the 19th century when thinking about the importance of the physical location of
Parliaments. David Owen has demonstrated that more goes on
in other arenas than in Westminster by the coverage he gets
outside the House. It is, for instance, irrelevant for the
BBC always to introduce the voting figures when reporting
Westminster since everyone knows they are irrelevant. In
the case of the European Parliament, where the institution
is weak, perhaps it would be better to concentrate on
reporting the work of the MEPs rather than the work of the
Parliament as a whole. It would be better to treat the
European Parliament as a special interest and to concentrate
on the work of the people in it rather than on the institution itself.

1. The Conservative Party - Brendan Donnelly, European Democratic Group

We have to draw a distinction between the attitude of the Conservative Party as a whole and the attitude of the Government. In general relations between the MEPs and the Government are good. The willingness of Ministers to see MEPs is almost an embarrassment. Their relationships are particularly close with the Foreign Office, which takes the Parliament more seriously than some other departments do. But it is not clear what response a Labour Government might make were it to be confronted with a sizeable majority of Conservatives in the European Parliament. There seem to be shared interests between the MEPs and the Government at present, but if the Conservative Party were not in power, relations between MEPs and the Government might be less happy. As far as the Party in general is concerned there is a less happy situation. It would be unfair simply to say that Central Office did not back up its European candidates, but there are deeper problems. These problems are fundamental to the British conception of the European Community itself, rather than just the role of the Parliament.

There are two basic difficulties in relations between Conservative MEPs and the rest of the party:

(1) The organisational anomaly of the European Constituencies makes it difficult for Conservatives to see them as an essential and integral part of the party and that party members have to do something about Europe as well as about Westminster. The Constituency base is a central element of party organisation, but the European Constituency has no identity.

(2) There are ambivalent attitudes to the European Parliament as an institution. Some Conservatives, while being out of the mainstream but not alone, consider the Parliament to be a risible institution and

that it could be a threat to freedom. Sometimes these two contradictory attitudes co-exist in the same person.

As far as the sovereignty argument is concerned the Parliament is part of this. In Britain sovereignty is not located in the people but in 'The Queen in Parliament'. But the European Parliament is a competitor for sovereignty with the Westminster Parliament. There are considerable worries about loss of sovereignty to Europe and the Conservatives in the European Parliament have not spelt out where the European Parliament fits into the sovereignty issue. I cannot see that the British Conservatives in the European Parliament have a future unless they form a vanguard of party thinking on this issue. Yet it is inevitable that if they do so they will be criticised for being too far along the road in respect of Europe. On the other hand this would provide them with a clearer public profile. We are too chary now, but if we were bolder people would understand where we stood. At present the Conservatives in the European Parliament have no clear role in the Conservative Party.

At a time of pressing economic and social questioning it is easy for the Parliament to fall into a back-water. It is too easy for it merely to acquire a sensationalised image of high-living to the exclusion of its more serious purpose. People have no idea what MEPs do, so trivial stories about the European Parliament are more worrying than similar stories of Westminster. The fact is that being an MEP is a useful job, but this is not fully echoed by the MEPs themselves.

Ann Robinson

The European Parliament tends to be a subject understood only by specialists. When canvassing people on doorsteps in the 1979 election, we found them totally ignorant of the Parliament and its role. Party activists were unable to rely solely on material for the election provided by Conservative Central Office. In order to put over the simple basic facts about the role of the Parliament it was necessary to use the material provided by the Community itself and also to produce specially simplified leaflets directed towards the interests of local people. In 1984 lack of in-

41

formation was not quite so great, but it was still necessary to promote the idea of the Community as a whole rather than the role of its elected Parliament. People in general still had little idea of what an MEP does. And the idea that the MEP, like his Westminster counterpart, represents, once elected, the interests of all his constituents of whatever party, has not yet sunk into the minds of some party activists. In areas represented by a Labour MEP there are many Conservatives who are unable to recognise him as being their MEP. Furthermore, some Conservative activists who will work hard for their Westminster Constituency will refuse to do anything for the European Constituency because they do not like the European Community at all. For example, we have found that some women have refused to join a newly-established branch of the European Union of Women (an organisation which has members in countries beyond the boundaries of the European Community) because they think that it is something to do with the European Community which they dislike.

2. The Labour Party - David Wilkinson, Hatfield Polytechnic (David Wilkinson worked for Labour Party Headquarters during the 1984 European Election Campaign)

It is useful to take as a starting point Ivor Crewe's five criteria for an ideal election. In the case of a European election it would be hoped that it would be on European issues and that the European Parliament would be the focus of the campaign. Labour, however, saw the European elections as the first international election and one that raised intriguing issues. Here we were choosing representatives with no formal responsibility for forming an executive government. It was hard, therefore, for parties to put forward detailed programmes or manifestoes. As a result the parties could campaign on any issues they wished whether European or non-European.

Secondly, since the creation of a majority in the European Parliament is not a vital consequence of the election, the objective of winning seats becomes of lower importance. The objectives are other than winning seats, they are to maximise the votes cast. In 1984 the Labour Party used these ambiguities to the full. Robin Cook, manager of the Labour campaign, said in December 1983 that the objectives were to establish Labour as the alternative to the Tories by beating the Alliance into third place. This could be done by obtaining the maximum number of votes rather than of seats. This strategy had consequences for the nature of the campaign and for how the European Parliament was to be presented during the campaign. If the objective was to win back votes then the issues on which the campaign was to be fought would have to be those which would fulfil this objective. A private poll conducted for the Labour Party showed that among these issues were unemployment and health care. Concentration on European issues would only lead to indifference among voters or to Thatcher winning since she was seen to be doing well for the UK in Europe. So the party managers decided that the European Parliament and issues should play no part in the campaign. The European election should be about Labour versus Thatcher, not about the European Community: it should be an ideological war based on Labour ideals. And, indeed, to concentrate on domestic issues proved a handy strategy for Labour since the European Community remained a sensitive issue within the party.

This approach had advantages and fostered unity within the party. But there were some influences working the other way, to prevent the election becoming a totally domestic campaign.

(1) The Labour Party, unlike the Conservatives, was deeply enmeshed in a transnational party organisation through its membership of the Socialist Group and the Confederation of Socialist Parties which produced a joint manifesto for the Election.

(2) The Conservatives had cornered the market in standing up for Britain's interests in Europe.

(3) The Labour Party was totally dependent on funds from the European Parliament for its campaign. It spent none of its own resources. So all of its publications had to acknowledge the Parliament and the money could not be used purely for national purposes and arguments.

(4) The British group of Labour MEPs had some influence on the campaign and on the way that it was run. For example,

Barbara Castle, Barry Seal and Alan Rogers were given seats on the European Campaign Group, the election steering committee. Barbara Castle was quite forthcoming in opposition to the campaign being run with a purely domestic emphasis. She made it clear that the European angle should not be ignored.

(5) Neil Kinnock was newly elected as party leader, with no ministerial experience, and the opinion polls showed that the public were aware of his lack of international experience, so he and Robin Cook were anxious that the campaign should not be entirely de-Europeanised. Kinnock was anxious to take the opportunity to be seen as an international statesman and he wanted to be associated with other Socialist leaders committed to an agreement on the joint manifesto of the Socialist Parties. He spoke to the European Parliament Socialist Group emphasising his commitment to Europe and was personally quite committed to getting the joint manifesto accepted.

So, in conclusion, although there were strong pressures from the National Executive Committee, particularly from the left, to play down the European aspects of the campaign, there were other contrary pressures that prevented that from happening completely.

Carole Tongue, MEP (London, East)

David has covered the party's role in the campaign from the Headquarters point of view and I shall distinguish the views of MPs, local activists, and trades unionists within the Labour Party. During the campaign I tried to talk directly about the Vredeling Directive in order to bring the Trades Union dimension to life and this had a certain success. My role as an MEP was more obvious to the Ford workers in the constituency than it was to the commuters.

The reaction of local activists to the campaign was mixed. My constituency was a marginal one with 48 per cent manual workers. It has six Tory and three Labour seats at Westminster, three of which are marginal. It was in the three marginals that there was the most positive response, and especially Wanstead and Woodford, a Conservative-held seat. There the activists saw the chance to have a Labour representative for the first time. In only two of the nine constituencies was there a totally negative response. In Newham North-East there was a council by-election so the excellent turnout there was more as a result of the fortuitous coincidence of the two elections. I was a trimming on the side there.

The MEP is still largely seen as the joker in the pack, not fitting clearly into the party structure. That is because there is a lack of knowledge about what our job really is about. People are much more concerned with local or national issues and they fail to see the international dimension of politics. I am on European Parliament Committees on the Environment and on Women's Affairs; both of these have a large body of legislation of direct relevance to all our constituents and I have been playing these topics up as much as I can.

There are some specific issues related to the car industry where the European dimension is important and where car industry trades unionists can appreciate the role of the MEP. These are (1) car pricing proposals and the threat of parallel imports, (2) lead in petrol, (3) exhaust emissions. And there has been a revival of interest in the Vredeling Directive. I have been invited to attend a meeting at Ford on the subject along with the local MP, Bryan Gould.

The most enthusiastic responses that I get from the party are still in the marginals like Wanstead and Woodford. At one recent meeting I presented an article I had written on 'Clearing the way for constructive European Community Debate'. At first this only resulted in closed eyelids but once I started talking about human rights and the moral reaction of the Community to South Africa and the Community's approach to Nicaragua they became more interested. I also described the Reagan visit to the European Parliament and the left-wing walk-out which interested them and everyone wanted to know exactly what had happened.

The response of the Parliamentary Labour Party and the Front Bench to the European Parliament has been varied. My own experience with people like Jo Richardson M.P. and Mr. David Clarke M.P. on the Environment has revealed that they do see a positive side to the Community.

There are ways to use the Community and its Parliament to political advantage. Bullets moulded in Strasbourg can be fired in the House of Commons and can be used to exert democratic control over the Ministers who take part in European decisions. I do not see how, under the present arrangements, the MEPs can control the Council of Ministers or the Committee of Permanent Representatives (COREPER): it is necessary to get to the Ministers before they leave for Brussels. If we are going to challenge them it is too late to wait until they get back from a meeting of the Council of Ministers. I am therefore trying to build up a positive liaison with MPs so that when a matter is discussed in Strasbourg I can get the information to Westminster so that it can be of use in influencing Ministers.

But among the Parliamentary Labour Party there is a certain amount of suspicion of the MEPs. I am in less danger of treading on MPs' toes than are those MEPs who have nine Labour MPs in their European Constituency. They tend to feel that they had better keep out of the way whereas I can do a European job and play a useful role by becoming an expert in the European Parliament and by getting involved in local campaigns. I can play the role of the MP and the local councillor because there are fewer Labour MPs in my constituency. However, I am careful not to indulge in Euro-speak or Euro-jargon if I want to get my message through. To get ideas over to people you do have to popularise the language and to clarify European issues and how the European Parliament relates to them in down-to-earth terms.

3. The Alliance Parties, Wendy Buckley, S.D.P. Headquarters

In the European election our objective of winning seats was not realised so the Headquarters office of the Alliance has had no continuing European role since the election. During the election campaign we presented a distinct pro-European stance. The Liberals had a long tradition of being in favour of the Community.

Ex-Labour members of the Social Democratic Party had left their original party because of their differences with Labour on Europe. Mrs. Thatcher had cornered the alternative of being in Europe but playing a tough nationalistic role. We tried to talk about issues which were relevant to ordinary people although the two parties had slightly different emphases. The SDP concentrated on jobs, industry, the European Monetary System, other economic issues and to some extent also security. The Liberal Party, for their part, were more interested in institutions and the Spinelli proposals for reform of the Community. Liberal internationalism ran through the European Liberal Group's manifesto.

During the campaign William Rodgers and Shirley Williams chose not to stand as candidates, reflecting the view that these were 'second order' elections (as Ivor Crewe indicated). But we ran a national campaign with leaflets, meetings, and national press conferences. We tried to be optimistic in a pessimistic climate. We put forward the urgency of European action on the economy, using the Albert and Ball report comparing US and European economies. But we failed to attract attention and got a low percentage of the votes cast and a low turnout. We mobilised those who were committed to the Alliance: the 18 per cent of votes cast for us demonstrated our bedrock support.

We tried to pitch our campaign in 1984 towards the issues of the next decade but it was very difficult, given that we were one year into the Thatcher government's second term. She had dictated British views about Europe. And the elite attitudes had changed since the 1960s. There are no longer so many pro-Europeans. So the SDP and the Liberals came out as rather old-fashioned, talking in terms of the social democratic approach of the 1970s. Many of the SDP activists had started out as activists in the referendum campaign for a 'Yes' vote and had been pro-European for decades. We should have tried to bring on more young people and have tried for a more modern image of Europe.

Another factor was that we could not get our voice heard, partly because of the outrageous chauvinism of the Conservatives; for example, the use of the D-Day 40th anniversary with double-page newspaper advertisements showing 40 years of peace, as part of the Conservative European election campaign. It was a simple popular message. We found it very difficult to get any other arguments into the arena.

The election was not sufficiently into the mid-term of the Government to mobilise a protest vote although Labour did succeed in this to some extent. And we also suffered from the effects of local elections in May and the Portsmouth South by-election on 8th June. We do not have a mass membership and our workers gave priority to the local elections and the by-election.

Finally, there was a lack of excitement to the campaign and no incentive to campaign on European issues. When we tried door-to-door campaigning we were made to feel like men from Mars. The party headquarters is now marginal to relations with the European Parliament because we have no members. We therefore do not choose to make issues in the European Community a feature of our politics unless they are central to domestic issues.

John Frears, SDP Councillor, Leicestershire

I have been involved in the 1975 referendum, and the 1979 and 1984 European Election campaigns. The referendum campaign was an exhilarating experience but as a grassroots activist I have to say how very disappointing the direct elections have been. They were a complete wash-out and a great disappointment. The result of the elections in the UK was a mockery as far as representation of public opinion is concerned, for these elections were simply regarded as a live opinion poll on the record of the Government of the day. The idea of democratic input to Europe means little to people in their everyday life. The public takes no interest in European Community issues.

Most of the work done by grassroots party activists is of a mundane nature - stuffing envelopes, addressing them and so on. It is hard to mobilise party workers for the European elections. The Alliance also had difficulty in raising funds; while the other parties had huge hand-outs from the European Parliament we got virtually nothing. We spend a great deal of time in addressing envelopes, but in other countries, France for example, the mailing is done by public authorities, as it was in the referendum when we did not have to do this. Without this task we could concentrate on the more interesting activities such as rallies and so on. In Leicestershire, for example, during the European elections there was no time for that sort of activity, as we were hard put to it just to distribute the basic leaflet to half a million voters.

Discussion

The history of successful parliaments is one of nominated parliaments with long agitation for democratic elections.

Perhaps the move to direct elections for the European Community has been premature. Perhaps it would be better to return to a nominated parliament and this might permit the better representation of special interests. Strasbourg is, after all, a focal point for interest groups. The dual mandate could be re-established or Strasbourg could adopt the model of the House of Lords, which might lead to a better assembly.

The problem with the European Parliament is its lack of relevance to the people. The election does not serve to elect an executive. And because of our particular electoral system we do not get out of the European Community what everyone else gets out of it. Six members of the European Parliament went home to become Foreign Ministers or Agriculture Ministers in their own governments. Four members were in the run-up to the French presidential election. Every single cabinet in Europe has someone in it who has experience of working alongside other nations in Europe. No-one in our cabinet has such experience. The Parliament is just a garage for people who are temporarily out of power. And we have had some unfortunate experiences with European Commissioners being national politicians sent out to garage. That is not a good idea for the future of the European Parliament.

Proportional representation is not the only alternative - for example there is the preferential vote system as used in Australia. It would be an advantage if we could change the electoral system: the Swedish and Australian examples could be considered as models. The problem with PR is choosing a system. Look at Ireland and compare the Labour Party results there in 1979 and 1984. Then there is the problem of how the parties would select those to include in the PR lists. These lists are in the hands of the party elite. A mixed system like that used in the Federal Republic of Germany might be the solution. There are advantages in keeping the single member constituency. One of the worst examples of the misuse of the list system occurred in Belgium where a Walloon nationalist was inserted into the Socialist list. He had never been a Socialist and this was duping the electorate. And some of the big names on the lists such as Marchais, Jospin and Mitterrand simply never turned up at the European Parliament. An attendance survey was carried out in the middle of the last Parliament. The British, Danes, Dutch and Luxembourgers were good attenders.

The French and Italians were poor. The Gaullists and the Communists were worst of all, although apart from that there was not much difference between the parties. Evidence about voters' turnout under different election systems is not encouraging. The IBA surveys indicate that the methods of election have little effect. And even if the number of voters did rise under PR the wasted votes would still occur.

Against the justice of proportional representation has to be put the fact that neither the Conservative nor the Labour Party would ever support the system even for elections to the European Parliament. The system would channel money to the Liberal/Alliance. It may be unjust but it is Labour Party policy to keep to our existing system of election.

The dual mandate is simply out of the question. It is impractical if the members are to do their job properly. An MEP cannot do two jobs. Campaigning goes on all the time. The impossibility of the dual mandate is demonstrated through the Economic and Social Committee model. The dual mandate creates representative poodles. But there are theoretically good arguments in terms of the European Parliament/National Parliament relationship. Therefore you do need to develop and foster a separate relationship between the two types of member in the two Parliaments. It has not yet been done successfully. In the UK there is jealousy of the Strasbourg facilities. And the MPs' fear that MEPs would clog up their tea-rooms and the library has prevented any institutional relationship being forged. Something needs to be done about this.

Conservative MEPs seem quite happy about their relationship with the Westminster MPs but they are not happy about Central Office - this emerged from the Normanton Report. The House of Commons is just like a public school and the MEPs are the day boys.

Some of the Labour MPs are still against the whole idea of the Common Market although some recognise particular advantages that the Community has brought. Jo Richardson, for example, has a knowledge of the work of the European Community on women's affairs. A Labour Party pamphlet in Jo Richardson's name covered the three Community Directives (on equal pay, equal treatment and equal treatment in social security). She has recognised that there is something valuable in Europe but still sees the Common Agricultural Policy as embodying the whole of the Community. There could be some simple changes without assuming any increase in the Parliament's powers.

(1) The Commission's proposals (on legislation for example) could come out as Green Papers as in the case of satellite TV. The consultation procedure could be more open and the Commission should list the bodies that they have consulted in the preparation of legislation.

(2) The Council of Ministers should be obliged to explain why they are not taking on board the Parliament's opinion.

(3) There should be more conciliation and concertation.

(4) There should be more access to what happens in COREPER.

All these measures could open up the institutions of the Community to a wider constituency of pressure groups. There are not all that many individual visitors coming to Strasbourg but MEPs see a lot of Trade Associations and there is immense lobbying in Strasbourg. MEPs do get correspondence from their constituents, from local authorities and businessmen with problems. There are not the individual cases that the Westminster MP gets.

As far as awareness of the Parliament's work is concerned the MEPs could take on a sort of Channel Tunnel initiative and hold meetings of members from France, Belgium and Luxembourg etc: There are issues in which more than one country has an interest, such as football. The Parliament must create its own publicity. What do MEPs intend to do now to ensure that they get a higher turnout next time?

There a number of issues that they could concentrate on, where MEPs know from their post-bags that there is wide public interest - such as seals, Ethiopia, car pricing, breast milk, the environment and consumer protection. There are items of real public interest such as acid rain, power stations, and so on. The campaign needs to start right now if there is to be a good turn-out in 1989. At present the majority of people see the Community in terms of agriculture or commerce. We need a proper common coal policy or a common energy policy and that would widen the interest.

Win Griffiths, MEP for South Wales

For me, one story sums up the feeling of the British electorate towards the European Parliament. In January 1986 I
was shopping in the Co-op when I heard an old woman discussing the purchase of material for a nightdress. She asked
the assistant 'Do you think a kilometre will be enough?'.
The answer came: 'It depends if you want to make it up with
sleeves or without'. There is similar misunderstanding when
people are talking about the European Parliament and what it
does.

For example, there is a belief about that members of
the European Parliament are directly responsible for giving
out grants from the European Regional Fund. Some people
simply do not believe that the Parliament does not give out
grants and as a member of its Regional Committee I am often
concerned with this question. The misunderstanding of our
role is one reason for the low turnout at European
elections. And in general there is a problem about how we
are viewed as elected members. After my first election to
the Parliament in 1979 my father was congratulated in my
home town of Brecon.   'Is that your boy who has been
elected to the European Parliament?' he was asked by interested friends. But by Christmas my father was saying to me
'Don't tell anyone that you are a member of the European
Parliament'. The argument about the British budget rebate
in Dublin and the action of the Parliament in blocking the
rebate had aroused hostility to the Community and its
Parliament. Mrs. Thatcher had played on all the nationalist
prejudices we have about the Community and its institutions.

My experience from two European elections is of a
fairly uniform national pattern, with Welsh exceptions.
Both the media and the national politicians set the scene
for the two elections, but from the inside there were some
experiences that give ground for optimism. Being a Labour
candidate for the European Parliament in 1979 just after a
general election defeat a few weeks earlier was like being a
general without an army. But the numbers of workers involved did not seem to affect the turnout. We found that
places which had not had all the leaflets distributed had a

similar turnout to those in which the leaflets had arrived. In the 1979 election the Party at the national level played no part at all except for the launch and printing of the manifesto. At the top of the party there was complete silence. I had six Labour members in my constituency and only one did anything at all to help me in the European campaign. Perhaps the others went out one day without telling me? This reflected the general level of participation. Publicity in the press, TV and radio was not too bad in 1979 considering that the European election took place directly after a general election. It was rather better in 1979, indeed, than it was in the 1984 election.

I had two great advantages on entering the European Parliament in 1979. I had no preconceptions about what the job would be like or indeed any idea about the whole operation of the European Community. That probably applied to most people elected in 1979. We have just got on and developed the job of MEP as we went along. For an MEP from South Wales there are more opportunities to get involved at the constituency level than there are for members from London and the South East. We make and receive representations on the Regional Fund, Social Fund, Coal and Steel Funds and all of these mean constituency involvement. There are no funds available for London MEPs to win for their constituencies so they have to get themselves involved in the legislative aspects of the Community such as consumer protection, the environment, and women's issues. It is hard to make an impact on these issues at home in the constituency and with the electorate. Carole's example of the Environment Committee is an example of a topic that the press ignored. People may be conned about the Social Fund but nevertheless this means good media coverage for the MEP. The MEP can become involved from time to time in the Regional Fund although in 90 per cent of the cases the application fits within the rules of the fund, is put in and considered by the two committees in Brussels made up of national civil servants who make the decisions. Applications need a two-thirds majority in the committee for acceptance by the Commission. If there is less than two-thirds the Commission can make its own decision. I can then come in to impress on the Commission the vital political importance of a project. In the case of the St. David's Conference Centre and Concert Hall in Cardiff the application was not accepted or rejected by the two-thirds majority rule. I, as local

MEP, was able to impress on the Commission that it was of vital importance to improve the image of the European Community in Wales.

In learning how the European Parliament worked I had my experience in local government to draw upon. That was true for many of the 1979 and 1984 intakes from the UK and there were also some ex-MPs from Westminster. The European Parliament works very much like local government with its plenary sessions every four weeks, dealing with Committee reports and preparatory group meetings before that. I was able to adapt to the system from the very beginning.

The European Parliament has one advantage over Westminster. We do have the opportunity in the Parliament to influence the Commission. The Commission is far more open to representations from the European Parliament than the UK Civil Service is to representations from Westminster MPs. To get into the UK Civil Service system you have to go to the Minister, but the MEP can go straight to the appropriate person in the Commission to make his representations. And European Parliament Committee members can get the Commission to accept their ideas for amendments at an early stage of the legislation, although it may take a long time for a result to emerge. For example, it took four years to get the proposals for steel crisis areas funds from the Regional Fund under which special consideration was given to Gwent and to South and West Glamorgan which have steel works closed or cut-back (Llanwern, Neath and Port Talbot). Special consideration was given in Gwent and to South and West Glamorgan because they were eligible through recent closures and cut-backs. But poorer mid-Glamorgan, with the highest unemployed level, was not included among the crisis areas. It did not qualify because it had no steel works located in its area. Eventually I got (with backing from the Parliament's Regional Committee) the Commission to include the travel-to-work area of the Port Talbot works which included mid-Glamorgan. This eventually went through and shows what MEPs can do. It became a Commission proposal, however, rather than a Parliamentary amendment and took two years for the Parliament to accept and another two years for the Commission to take it on board. Before the 1984 election I became very involved in constituency work. I produced reports to the Labour Party so that when we got to the 1984 election the Labour Party activists were aware of the work of the European Parliament and were more prepared to get involved in the campaign. They were also motivated by the start of Mrs. Thatcher's second term and a year's rest from campaigning and the huge defeat of 1983 which they wanted to erase. So if the Labour Party was to recover a credible position in UK politics it had to start with the European election. We had quite an army of support. Although it was not fought like a general election campaign there were press conferences, and the Labour Party organised six regional Euro-Festivals in which prominent European political personalities took part. In Wales we had an eve-of-poll rally in which Willy Brandt took part. But it was not covered by the media.

The party leadership did get involved, including Neil Kinnock, and there was a will to see that we did well in the 1984 election. But compared with general or even local elections there was not a uniform level of activity in all seats. In my own constituency the ratio of Westminster MPs between the two major parties was 3:6 Conservative to Labour in 1979 but by 1983 it was 5 Conservative to 4 Labour. On paper my majority might have been about 3,000. So the seat was, in theory, winnable for the Conservatives. Fortunately for me the Labour party was more active in the election and the turnout was up for us. There was also the reaction to the Conservative general election victory and to the miners' strike. But there must have been some other reason why turnout increased in Wales overall. There was not the same effect in South Yorkshire so there must have been some other reasons. There's a paper in this for some political scientist.

After 1979 relations with the MPs in my constituency were cordial but more or less at arm's length. The European MP is the last home of all lost causes: I sometimes receive a letter from an MP asking me to deal with a problem that he knows is insoluble... and asking 'Is there possibly a European dimension to this?'. But relations have got better over time and in the 1984 election all the Labour MPs got involved in the campaign and at least put in an appearance.

One of the things you have to get used to about being an MEP is the idea that people in general are not aware of your existence. If they were they would invite you to do things for them. Of the local authorities some are clued in and do contact me regularly. Other local authorities forget that I could help them. As for the media, the BBC do a pretty good job on the news side but on the more general current affairs programmes they rarely have MEPs. The local BBC show Meet for Lunch never asks the local MEPs to appear - they only ever have a London-based MEP (originally from Wales).

The fact that other legislatures have had to fight for their right to a share of political power or to be democratically elected may make a difference to the way in which they are perceived by the general public. They have more status. But this is not the situation of the European Parliament. Any transfer of power to it will have to come from another elected body, not direct from the people. In the long term, provided that the European Community can overcome its current crises of enlargement, the budget and agricultural prices how will the institutions respond? I take the optimistic view, even though it looks as though this year the Community might become bankrupt. There has to be major reform of the institutions if the European Community is to have credibility with the electorate, and if the electorate is to become involved in the process of choosing their representatives. It is the Community that has to change, not so much the Parliament. The question is whether MEPs will be prepared to stick it out during this long term process in what is after all a difficult job with low recognition, while turnout in elections is declining. I have a certain optimism. It must change for the better but I cannot guarantee that the MEPs will stay on to fight the good fight. There is no real cohesion on party lines in the European Parliament. On issues such as reform of the CAP the Parliament splits on national lines. These splits are difficult for the media to report. I make some pleas to the media. You are improving the coverage of the Parliament on TV and radio but not in the national press. There is too much trivialisation of news...even The Guardian could produce trivial headlines such as: 'Yes, it's true Brussels wants your blood'. This headline about research plans simply played upon existing British anti-European prejudices.

Discussion

Win Griffiths ought to have complained to the local BBC Radio Wales producer who did not use Welsh MEPs on his programme. The BBC does not keep a central register of contributors, but each individual producer decides who goes on. The MEPs could demand a meeting with the Controller, Radio Wales. After all, an elected person is something holy: you would certainly be given an audience. You must push, no-one else will do it for you. You are fighting on radio and TV for a very little space and the producers need a balance of views. So the pressure from you people is justified and from the media point of view the same people are used time and time again because they are known quantities and reliable. You are expecting too much if you expect that the press and the broadcasters will come to meet you. Publicity has to be earned. And it is innocent not to do anything to ensure that you are used as much by local BBC radio as other MPs and MEPs. It is necessary to do some self-promotion. It is essential for the MEP to be professional at this aspect of his work. He must become a self-publicist. But he must also guard against the possibility of becoming a 'Rent-a-Quote'. He must fit into the well-managed stratum between the two extremes. After all, which MEPs do we remember? We remember Barbara Castle as being forceful and John Prescott (a member of the pre-elected Assembly) for his hard work on the fisheries issue and what a good job he did on it: we remember the pictures of John Prescott together with British fishermen.

Some people have been in favour of a directly-elected Parliament but now look back wistfully to the nominated members like Peter Kirk and John Prescott who were much more effective than the directly-elected MEPs. Without the dual mandate the maintainance of civilised and friendly relations is difficult and leads to a low level of clout for MEPs at Westminster. MEPs have more clout with the Civil Service than they do with politicians. The attitude of the parties at national level seems to be: if MEPs are powerful stirrers, 'Boo', but if they are doing a good job as ombudsmen, 'Hurrah'.

At the time of the budget rebate decision there was an argument on the vote to block the budget rebate to Britain about whether we should put the rebate on the revenue or the expenditure side of the budget. The Labour MEPs wanted the money to be spent in the regions on the capital spending side, and opposed Mrs. Thatcher's argument that the money should be allocated to the revenue side. Regionalists wanted it on the expenditure side, but purists wanted it on the revenue side. If the Labour Party had been in government there might have been some friction between it and its MEPs.

But although there was good coverage of the Parliament's rejection of the 1984 Budget by the Financial Times elsewhere the coverage was thin.

The Labour MEPs had little effect on Walworth Road and the leader's office between 1979 and 1984 when they were only 17 in number and were committed to withdraw from the Community at the first opportunity. Now there is more dialogue between the 32 MEPs and the party leadership, principally between Barbara Castle and the leadership, and there are more shadow spokesmen coming to Strasbourg and Brussels to discuss matters with a European angle. Also now under the re-selection process, MEPs have been asked not to stand for Westminster seats where there is a sitting MP.

We have attacked the media but the problem may lie with the Parliament, which has few teeth but strong gums. Its procedures are not clear. First of all no one knows where we have got to in the decision-making process when a Committee issues a report. Secondly some MEPs are opportunists who focus on trivial items like the tattoo-ing of cats and dogs. Some MEPs, as well as the media, want to trivialise what the European Parliament does. MEPs tend to latch on to one issue to make a name for themselves.

The first of these problems, that there is no discernable outcome from the Parliament's work, causes confusion and makes it harder for the media to cover the Parliament. As there is no sense of power the media look for the fun stories like Waterloo Station and they do get coverage. There is also an element of cultural clash of expectations associated with the word Parliament. We should go back to calling it an Assembly. It does not help, either, to use the Parliament as a moral forum to discuss matters over which it has no competence, such as the Middle East.

Most current affairs producers feel that if they are going to apply time, personnel and resources to a story it must have significance to the people who will receive it. These are sound journalistic principles. There is no sense that the Parliament is a significant political institution.

If you make news it will be reported. People are interested in trivial news. News is a random process and you cannot predict when a story will catch fire.

There are MEPs who will not bother to do anything about issues unless they obtain publicity for their actions. But others know that action pays off in the long run. Win Griffiths gave an example of long-term effects. About a year ago he asked the Commission if they were satisfied with the way that Britain was applying the Directive on Bathing Water. He was hoping to find some way to acquire money from the Regional Fund to clean up the beaches of South Wales. The Commission replied that they were having discussions with the UK authorities and would, if necessary, be taking the British Government to the Court of Justice for infringement of the Directive. And they also said that they would consider requests for grants from the Regional Fund to clean up beaches. By January he had heard nothing about the outcome of the Commission's talks with the British Government and put down further questions. By that time there were reports in the Welsh press about the poor state of the Welsh beaches, and about the way in which the UK had applied the Community directive. Eventually he got a reply from the Commission saying that someone had complained to them about the UK's application of the Directive and then suddenly he got on to John Craven's Newsround, and the Jimmy Young Show, Breakfast Time TV ran a film on the subject and Watchdog rang up for information. Yet this story had been fed into the weekly papers and none of them took it up. Some other things that the MEP does, however, get no reaction. It may be that some succeed by following the example of Woodrow Wyatt, who cleverly supplied two-line quotes to the Press Association every day. He put in more stories than his party leader, Clem Attlee. John Ling used to be good like this, and Richard Cottrell works at it all the time. Good publicity does not come by chance.

Carole Tongue, however, slogged away trying to get publicity on the relationship between the European wine lake and alchoholism but another MEP got the Perrier Water story which got picked up for the front page although he had not planned the publicity.

It was pointed out that publicity is not the prime end of an MEP's life. The 'rent-a-quote' MPs are often laughed at. Woodrow Wyatt was an exception. Superficial publicity-mad MPs are often bad MPs. There are other things that MEPs can do. If they are unable to do much constituency work they can take up an agenda-setting role on the basis of vainglory or because they have a licence to be heard. Enoch Powell is an example of this type of member. But the Powell type of campaign might not apply to controversial issues in the European Parliament.

The media are not in the business of publicity but in the business of reporting things of significance. The media cannot act as the publicity arm of any institution. But an agenda-setting role could be a significant one for the European Parliament. One role of the media is to amplify certain arguments and thoughts. If you take the flow of information coming into any news organisation with seven wires per day, it would require all of six days to read the daily output of any one of them. There is a great pressure of news coming in so it is necessary to select and priority setting is difficult. The MEPs see the role of the media as to help promote various philosophies and strategies but the media, for their part, sees their business as reporting. The audiences for the different media overlap, but the media are engaged in reporting first and foremost. On the other hand, the role of the MEP is to make political statements. In Enoch Powell's case it was not by chance that he made his 'rivers of blood' speech in Birmingham where the TV could report it. Macmillan's 'winds of change' speech was first made in Accra where it was missed by the media who were alerted when he made it again in Johannesburg. The media do not like being used, but the MEPs are in the business of using the media.

People do like silly stories. Twice Gallup has run surveys about the books that people keep in their bathrooms and about the decor of their bedrooms - black sheets and so on. These surveys were commissioned by a paint company and everyone picked it up as a good story.

The Parliament, if it wants publicity for its efforts, must put out stories that get away from the trivialising stereotype many of the media have of the Parliament. The looney story is sought by the press because it is expected. There is much inconsistency in the behaviour of the media. Some stories get taken up and others, equally good, are rejected. The popular press, in particular, does trivialise the Parliament and the Community as a whole by using stories that they would not print were they to emanate from Westminster but which they use because they come from those funny guys across the channel.

It is important to remember that the purpose of the popular press is to sell newspapers and to make money, not to educate. On the old Daily Mirror they used the yardstick 'What are they going to talk about in the pubs tomorrow?' and in the old Daily Mirror there was some attempt to raise the people's sights - but then The Sun came along and sold more copies and The Mirror lost its nerve. And the quality newspapers are not doing all that much better. The fact is that Fleet Street exists to make money.

SESSION SIX: THE EUROPEAN PARLIAMENT IN THE EYES OF THE PARTY ACTIVISTS

Pamela Entwistle, Conservative Party and the Kangaroo Group.

I have one overriding memory of the European election last year. A clear bright morning - hardly anybody on the streets - the campaign truck, bedecked with ribbon, passing a crematorium. The candidate was repeating over and over 'Vote for a strong voice in Europe - Vote for me'. And as we passed that crematorium I thought we have about as much hope of alerting the people in the constituency as we have of convincing the spirits of the people in the crematorium.

But you have asked me to talk on how the party activists see the European Parliament. A generous estimate would I think be that some 3 per cent of those who play an active part in their Westminster constituency parties are interested in Europe or want to help. And whilst loyalty would prevent them from saying so they think of the European Parliament as remote, bureaucratic and over-staffed. They think of food mountains and interference with national policies, and of their MEPs as going off on exciting trips abroad once a week.

I have, over the past six years, worked on four election campaigns. During the first direct European elections in 1979 I worked with the European League for Economic Co-operation and with them travelled the country organising seminars to talk to those going out supporting candidates. The seminars started in January some six months before the election and slowly the interest started to build up. At the end of April we were estimating a turn-out of the electorate of 60-65 per cent and this was supported by expert psephologists.

Then the General Election was announced and Europe became an appendage to national politics, and there it has stayed.

In 1983 I worked in the General Election campaign in Hornchurch, a Tory marginal, and there to my surprise among the many traditional Labour supporters found that one of the major issues raised on the doorstep was that we needed to be a part of the European Community - and that whilst they may have voted against our continued membership at the time of the referendum they were now committed to our remaining in membership.

By 1984 European politics was once again an extension of national and local politics - particularly in Central London where I worked for the three weeks of the campaign, starting at 7.30 in the morning and going through to 10 o'clock at night. I had only one question on anything that might be vaguely European - 'How do you convert metres to yards?' - and I suspect that that was from someone who was cutting out a dress.

Certainly there were lots of statements like 'We pay too much'. The 'give us our money back' campaign had done nothing to make us feel European. There were statements like 'Why do we give butter to the Russians?' and 'They sell more to us than we do to them'. Then there were the statements that fuelled the 'anti-European' 'Buy British' campaign like 'I always buy British' and 'They are taking away our jobs' and so on. The electors had read these things in the newspapers so they had to be true, didn't they?

I have a theory that every journalist moved from the town to the country over those three weeks. They started off in their town houses complaining that all Brussels wanted to do was to harmonise lawnmower noise - and if any of you have had your Sundays disturbed by the neighbour mowing his lawn you might see the point of harmonising lawnmower noise. Then they all rushed off to the country and joined Barbara Castle's criticisms that all Brussels did was to try to harmonise vacuum cleaner noise. Not a bad thing if you live in a flat with a noisy neighbour upstairs. The real issue behind these apparently silly proposals is that we need to sell in other countries so we must have standards which suit their market. Yet there is no media or political consciousness that this is the reason.

During the campaign when we were calling on voters, even committed Conservatives, to ask them to vote for the Conservative European Candidate they would say 'Oh, Peter Brook's my member', or 'Geoffrey Finsberg's my member'. There was absolutely no identification with the Euro-Constituency and no comprehension that their vote in a safe Westminster seat was needed to balance the marginal areas or Labour strongholds in the larger European seat.

It is easy to criticise, but that is what I am going to do, though I hope then finally to put forward one or two thoughts on how we might improve public involvement next time round.

The referendum campaign was well-organised but its promises of increased prosperity, like that experienced by the six founder-members, was doomed by the oil crisis. The public rightly felt let down. And the Britain in Europe campaign organisation having been disbanded after the referendum, there was no all-party organisation in a position to respond.

As I said earlier, the 1984 election campaign was fought on domestic issues. In London the overriding interest was in the abolition of the Greater London Council. None of the leading politicians did anything to raise the level of debate to the really important European issues which are:

of changes to make European decision-making more effective;

of completing the European internal market;

of opening up the markets in services;

of the benefits of the Fisheries Policy - my fishmonger knew it was a good thing, but no politician ever said so;

of the European Monetary System;

of mutual recognition of qualifications;

of worker representation on boards;

of ways of extending the Youth Training Schemes to cover spending some time in another member state;

of saving the consumer £7 billion a year by stopping frontier delays and making it easier for us to travel.

No, they did not talk about any of these things. They just responded to statements made by their opponents and repeated the phrase 'Fair Shares for Britain'.

Did the leading politicans assume that we would not understand? Did they think that raising the level of discussion would affect their level of popularity in the polls? Or cynically did they want the election to be kept quiet in the hope that this would help their chances?

Whatever the reasons we must start now to get a greater understanding of European policies and issues. Here we have a lot to learn from the United States, where the constituencies are roughly the same physical size and contain the same numbers of voters as those of the European

Parliament. In my political party I would like to see a campaign steering committee set up in each of the Euro-Constituencies now. These would be steering committees containing experts on communications and on issues affecting the particular constituency. And I mean experts and not just people with political ambitions of their own.

I would also like to see free mailings once a year to every voter so that the member can tell all his electorate what he is doing and why, as is done in the States. As it is, were I not already involved in European politics I would not have known that Stan Newins was my member. I would like to see the members linked directly to their constituencies by computer from their offices in Brussels and Strasbourg, so as to be able to respond quickly and inform the electorate on what is going on in Europe. I would like us to look at the ways in which we select our candidates. Perhaps the party members would feel more involved if we went to a system like the American primaries?

I would like to see politicans telling us the facts straight. If we need to have VAT on food in order to have a Common Market (and that would mean a lower rate on other things) they should have the courage to say so. If we need to have a common electoral system to make European elections fair, then say so. If we need to come closer to our European partners through European Union, then let them say so. The politicians should initiate discussion. There is very little in the press here about Europe, in comparison with coverage in Germany, Italy and France.

Finally, we need to look at our methods of campaigning. Trying to knock on doors in a constituency the size of Central London does not work. Holding public meetings for 20 of the party faithful and 10 selected members of the opposition does not work. Asking people to advertise with window bills (which they are increasingly reluctant to do) does not work. And one - yes one - bedecked campaign vehicle for the area of Central London does not work. We must look urgently at new ways of reaching the electorate through the media. A 25 per cent poll does not contribute to making the Community more democratic.

I will turn now to the Kangaroo Group in the Parliament, which is not yet three years old and is already supported by 150 MEPs, the Commission and some member governments. It presses for the free movement of people and goods, trying to eliminate the £7 billion of wasteful costs each year caused by the present system. It also aims to achieve one set of European standards, although the group now thinks that recognised standards bodies throughout Europe should be accepted as it is taking too long to harmonise all standards.

The Kangaroo Group issues a bi-monthly newsletter in several languages. Kangaroo goes to 40,000 people and is sent by courier to news editors and leading politicians. But the press shows little interest. At a dinner and conference held at the Institute of Directors with participants including Sir Geoffrey Howe, Lord Cockfield, Wisse Decker and Basil de Ferranti, only one member of the press was present although all had been invited. The Financial Times published a story about the event in its European edition only. Yet several news-worthy items had been aired at the event. The Kangaroo Group is also involved in the production of three information films by independent television companies. One of these will be a Panorama-type programme on the Community, the second will be a 'Press-Call' featuring interviews with Brussels-based journalists, and the third will be a 'human interest' documentary on the life of a Euro-politician.

Discussion

Pressure needs to be put on the government to supply some form of state support for mailings to constituents, for this is expensive. Electoral mail should be distributed by the local authorities on behalf of the parties as is done in France. On the other hand, some parties have done very well under the existing arrangements for European election funding, and this includes the major British parties.

If the next elections to the European Parliament were to be conducted under some form of proportional representation this would entail a very different form of campaigning. It might also increase the significance of local and regional media authorities and get a more interested electorate.

If there is to be more appeal to the general electorate then the language used to describe issues needs to be considered in order to reduce wide, abstract and laden ideas to ordinary language. Community issues need to be translated down so as to be taken from the intellectual sphere to the imaginative sphere. The stereotypes and the Euro-bread,

Euro-beer and so on are also not helpful.

An enormous difference exists between London and rural Euro-constituencies both during the actual election campaigns and between them. It is harder for London MEPs to get known through the local press. Although there is a key role for the regional TV: the idea of buying time did not overcome the problems of reaching large numbers of people.

The IBA viewing figures for 1984 showed that about 30 per cent felt that coverage of the election had been 'about right': 19 per cent thought there was too little and only 16 per cent thought there had been too much. This compared with 71 per cent who thought that there had been too much coverage of the 1983 General Election. A close observer of elections for thirty years recalled that 1984 was the only election he had seen where there was declining public interest during the campaign. An outstanding fact was that the Daily Star had made no reference to the campaign whatever during its last eight days (and had only made three references in total). Brian Walden had said that he would not cover the European Election in Weekend World.

It was suggested that the Kangaroo Newsletter and similar literature had to be sent to the right named individual on a newspaper or radio station; if it were merely sent to the news editor it would tend to be sent on to the sports editor. It was difficult for a radio station to carry a general story more than once or twice a year (that is a story of the 'Oh-er' kind), for listeners would note the repetition and get bored.

One month before the General Election and the European Election in 1979 ITN were convinced that there was not enough coverage and this was confirmed by surveys of attitudes taken after the European election. This prompted a major effort to rectify the situation for 1984. A survey on election day showed that 70-73 per cent had seen something about the election on TV (1984 Harris Poll showed 83 per cent). In fact actual coverage is not so much less in Britain than elsewhere. The problem with Europe is that the time-scale of its decisions and issues is so long. The TV news cannot do more than one item each year on lorries or something like that. In the Community policy changes take ten years to develop. But focus, relevance and timing are the key factors for TV coverage.

FINAL SESSION: SUMMARIES OF PARTICIPANTS' VIEWS

Norman Webb would be pleased to get reactions to Eurobarometer and would like suggestions for making it more useful that he could pass on to the Commission. Some of the Eurobarometer questions have already been discussed with MEPs but one problem about new developments was that Eurobarometer was short of money. To some extent the media have been 'stonewalling', saying that their business is to report news not to promote the Parliament. This leaves a lot of room for judgement about their coverage of the Parliament and there may be a certain bias creeping in of an untraceable kind.

Colin Seymour-Ure pointed to the difference between the publicity needs of the European Parliament as an institution and those of MEPs. The MEPs have options as to the role that they shall play; they can act as welfare officers (which they may find depressing or fulfilling) or they can aspire, say, to an agenda-setting role. They cannot avoid the lobbyist role. The publicity needs of each of these roles are different. It is axiomatic that no-one gets the publicity they want, not even sportsmen.

By comparison with individuals the publicity needs of organisations are autonomous. Parliament as an institution has few options. So long as it is a marginal institution of limited interest to the general public, publicity is bound to be random, unpredictable, and perverse. We should not think of The Sun and The Star as newspapers: they do not need to come out every day. The significance of the response of the specialist media is therefore greater whether they are specialised by subject, geographical location or audience/customer.

Paul McKee said that the word used most by his colleagues to describe news coverage of the European Parliament was 'relevance' and they find little of relevance in the activities of the European Parliament. MEPs do not have a sharp focus on either the aim and procedures of the Parliament or on their own activities. There is a lot of learning entailed as MEPs search for their role. They will have to put themselves into sharper focus which would make them ap-

68

pear more 'relevant'. ITN has now moved away from European activities towards a stronger emphasis on: individual events in European countries; their industrial and social policies and their politics which is more relevant to our viewers. This gives them a wider eye on Europe than they had ten years ago. In the next 5-7 years there will be a transformation in TV and radio 'ecology' through the proliferation of local stations, satellite and cable channels and so on. The advent of Channel 4 is a minor step to what will happen in the next few years. For the past 35-40 years broadcasting time has been scarce, but now this is changing so priorities of programme makers will change. Opportunities will exist there for the MEPs if their activities can be brought into sharper focus.

David Butler was not sure that we have not agonised too much about lack of publicity for the European Parliament. Many political institutions, such as Oxfordshire County Council, get very little publicity, so we should relax a bit.

John Eidinow thought that MEPs are rather like the US soldiers in the second world war who were 'overpaid, overfed and over there'. He was surprised to find that the European Parliament is not doing too badly for publicity. But if cuts are made to radio services then coverage of the European Parliament might suffer. He was impressed by the MEPs present at the seminar and by their commitment and hard work. But he saw a rhetoric gap. The Parliament puts out a film entitled 'Having our Say', but the Parliament does not have its say. MEPs have done very well for publicity against the general background of the poor state of the European Community and its institutions. They all need a good public relations agency. It is important that MEPs direct their stories to named individuals in the media; that they clarify their role and their parliamentary procedures; and that they look at the range of topics that they cover - some are more relevant to people than others. They should not divert their energies across too wide a field, for this only devalues the Parliament. The Parliament should not be considering Northern Ireland but the European environment and acid rain and toxic waste. We should drop the word "Europe" and talk about the European Community, for that is what we want to build, after all.

Nigel Hawkes said that we should refer to the European Community and not to the EEC. He answered the charge that correspondents covering European Community topics were stonewalling. They are more interested in the European Community than the average pressman, but cannot proselytise for the European Idea. Correspondents have some credit with news editors but cannot draw upon it for ever. Journalists don't write about subjects, they write stories. It is not possible to write about a subject without a story: there has to be at least some advance, some peg, on which to construct a piece. People should bear this in mind when issuing press releases.

Paul Hodgson referred to the insular atmosphere of the discussions that had taken place at the seminar. The rhetoric was different in continental Europe although, in fact, things were not much better there. We have not done so badly in Britain even compared with France, so we should not despair. Some groups elsewhere in Europe are more hostile to a European Community than those in Britain. There has been a withdrawal of internationalist feeling and there is less quality press and broadcasting interest in foreign affairs than formerly was the case. This retreat from international feeling is not peculiarly British. The correspondent of Le Monde, who has worked three times in London, now found that less of what he sent back was being published. On several occasions he had to argue to get his material published. The power has moved to Washington and Moscow. When people like Brian Walden start talking about 'Eurobore' it becomes a fashion which is hard to stop. It's fashionable to say 'no-one understands the CAP' and that creates an excuse not to bother or to make the effort to explain complexities. How this vicious circle is broken he did not know.

Roger Morgan disagreed with John Eidinow about those subjects which the European Parliament ought not to cover: subjects like Northern Ireland and the Middle East. The problem is the way in which the European Parliament takes these subjects up. The European Parliament is not a legislature and does not make day-to-day policy. This was true before direct elections. It could make a virtue out of necessity by using its research staff, contacts and resources and holding hearings to produce reports on real issues, such as the Albert and Ball report on the economy.

It could then make an impact with its reports much as the House of Lords does with those it produces. This would lead to more attention from the media.

Ann Robinson pointed out that certain procedures of the committees of the European Parliament prevent the reports from being as useful as they might be because they do not contain evidence from outside sources and experts as do the House of Lords reports. The reports from the European Parliament's committees are merely statements. If the Parliament wants to get more enmeshed in the policy process it must provide well-supported arguments to support the policy positions that it takes.

Win Griffiths referred again to the greater need for British MEPs for personal publicity to attract votes under the single member constituency system. Members from other countries using the list system only have to maintain their position in the party list. British MEPs have a very personal interest in what is reported about the Parliament. His main concern was with the inconsistency of coverage by the media. There are many different pressures on the media and those MEPs who had attended the seminar had picked up some useful tips on how to approach the media.

It is not clear whether the Parliament should concentrate on debating Commission proposals on which it can take some action or whether it should tackle topics over which it has no power or real influence. Here the Parliament faces one of its fundamental problems vis-a-vis reporters. Once the Parliament has given an opinion on Commission proposals that is not the end of the story. It may be one year or eighteen months before any action is taken. There are 400 items on which opinions have been given by the Parliament that are still awaiting Council approval. An example of one of these is the change in the Regional Fund regulations originated by himself.

Win Griffiths also wondered what the media would think of the proposal to move to votes immediately after the debate on all issues before the Parliament. As a Vice-President of the Parliament and a member of the Executive Committee concerned with reporting he would welcome ideas from the media for improvements. Among current proposals was the permanent manning in Strasbourg of the Parliament's publicity and radio facilities (at present the staff of the publicity centre are located in Luxembourg). As things are now the facilities are little used.

Carole Tongue wished to echo the sentiments expressed by Win Griffiths. She appreciated the problems caused for the media by the Parliament's procedures. No-one ever knows what stage a proposal is at. It is the Council of Ministers that is blocking the 400 items of legislation in Brussels. The Parliament ought to be able to call the Council to task and ask 'Why have you not decided this issue?' But the Council steals the limelight and you end up thinking that the Council has done all the work. Some public funding is required for MEPs to inform constituents - a yearly newsletter alone costs about £4,000 a time. There should also be better liaison between the MEPs and their party leaders. Those at the top, Kinnock and Thatcher, don't like to publicise the European Community. Finally, Carole Tongue thought that there should be more seminars like this so that MEPs and media can help each other.

Roger Broad thanked the participants for coming to Wiston House for the seminar. It had improved his morale no end. He saw three main points for action emerging from the discussions. Firstly, there was a procedural question. So many items get put onto the agenda of the European Parliament and then some have to be dropped at the last moment. That is very frustrating for a journalist who may have come specially to Strasbourg. Secondly, the Parliament fails to follow through the decisions that it has taken and it could come back much more often to the Council on the 400 items that have been held up in Brussels and pursue them (for example in Question Time) to find out which country is responsible for holding up the decisions. At the moment the media excuse their own governments when they engage in blocking action. Thirdly, the money for elections should be better spent. The £600,000 allocated for television advertising in 1984 was a waste. Too little was spent, and in the wrong way. Perhaps the Parliament should pay for an annual mailing to local authorities, trades councils and other constituency opinion formers and channels. The institutional changes agreed at the December 1985 summit give Parliament the chance to pursue these problems but they also challenge Parliament itself to pursue a more consistent approach to major policy issues.

CONCLUSION

Ann Robinson

At the start of this conference we expressed the hope that it might, by revealing the sources of the present poor public image of the European Parliament, show us how to improve it. There is no doubt that the European Parliament has a poor public image and a poor press in the UK (although many participants pointed out that this country is not unique in this respect). The poor image of the Parliament seems to be inextricably linked to the poor public appreciation of the European Community itself. Evidence from Eurobarometer, however, indicates that the people of Europe are largely in favour of the broad idea of European integration, and are less antagonistic than the low turnout at the European elections in 1979 and 1984 indicates.

Many participants pointed out that we have to look to the attitudes of political elites - party leaders particularly - if we are to understand the roots of the Parliament's poor image. The image of the European Community and its Parliament, as displayed during the course of two European Elections, was deliberately blurred by political leaders and national parties who chose to fight those elections on national issues. The attitude of party leaders filters right down to the grass-roots activists. The low turnout for the elections and the lack of coverage of the elections by the media is, therefore, a reflection of the lack of enthusiasm displayed by political leaders. There was general agreement that so long as the national Governments and party leaders fail to encourage a European outlook the Parliament will continue to have a hard time attracting the attention of both voters and the media. Because a European election does not produce a Government, it appears somewhat irrelevant, particularly in British eyes. Power in the Community remains concentrated in the hands of the member states in the Council of Ministers and the Summits. National Governments do not want to surrender power to the Community or to draw attention to its Parliament.

The media, like the voters, pay little attention to a weak institution. The media are interested in reporting power and action and there is limited news value in a

73

peripheral institution. The Parliament, however, must take its share of the blame for its poor media coverage. It concentrates its efforts too often on those issues which are not its direct concern and misses issues which it could cover.

The European Parliament is a hard institution to report. There is no obligation for routine coverage as in the case of a national legislature. There are few good personalities among the members; the Parliament moves around from place to place and the cost of coverage is high; it has confusing procedures; and, most importantly, there is a lack of definition about its work and role. Only in those regions where there has been a considerable amount of Community funding is there evidence of more, and more positive, media coverage of the Community and of its MEPs.

The participants from the parties supported the view expressed by academics and the media representatives that their leaders and headquarters do not back up MEPs and the Parliament. The UK MEPs are not integrated into the mainstream party and political machinery. Because the European Community and its Parliament are seen as competitors for sovereignty they must therefore be kept well under control. However, there is much that individual MEPs can do to promote the role of the Community and publicise its impact on people's everyday lives by concentrating on those many European issues that have direct relevance to the individual citizen. As one of the MEPs present said, the MEP has 'to clarify European issues' and to point out to people how 'the European Parliament relates to them in mundane terms'.

The conference participants agreed that there is a need for a change of attitude among the leaders of the main UK political parties so that they take the Community more seriously and cease using European elections as tests of national popularity. There needs to be better liaison between MEPs and their parties and some regular public funding in order better to inform constituents of community matters. For its part, Parliament has to settle itself in a permanent home together with other Community institutions, to improve its own procedures and make them easier to report and to consider its own proper role and concentrate on promoting the real European issues of today and tomorrow. There are indeed many such issues, including the internal market, the environment, acid rain, toxic waste, consumer protection, car pricing, equal pay, and political co-operation. The recommendations of the conference participants point a way forward for the Parliament, even if national Governments are unwilling to afford it greater direct power. MEPs who wish to see the Community and its Parliament with a better, clearer public image and a better coverage in the media have to make what they do more relevant to the voters, and thus to the media. The public image of any political institution is determined ultimately by its own actions. The way forward for the European Parliament is surely for it to concentrate its efforts on those issues, and to work in those ways, that ensure that it is regularly and well reported. Only then can it look forward to a better image among the voters and higher turnout at European elections.

STUDIES IN EUROPEAN POLITICS
Published by the Policy Studies Institute

This series provides brief and up-to-date analyses of European political issues, including developments in the European community and are in transnational political forces, and also major problems in particular European countries. The series is edited by the Head of the Centre, Dr. Roger Morgan. The research is undertaken by the European Centre for Political Studies, established in 1978 at the Policy Studies Intitute with the sponsorship of the European Cultural Foundation.

SEP 1 **The Future of the European Parliament**
David Coombes (May 1979, pp.136) £3.95

SEP 2 **Towards Transnational Parties in the European Communty**
Geoffrey and Pippa Pridham (May 1979, pp.26) £1.80

SEP 3 **European Integration, Regional Devolution and National Parliaments**
David Coombes, L. Condorelli, R. Hrbek W.Parsons, S. Schuttemeyer (July 1979, pp.45) £2.25

SEP 4 **Eurocommunism and Foreign Policy**
Carole Webb (November 1979, pp.81) £2.95

SEP 5 **Europe Elects its Parliament**
Genevieve Bibes, Henri Menudier, Francoise de la Serre, Marie-Claude Smouts (September 1980, pp.69) £2.50

SEP 6 **The European Voter: Popular Responses the First Community Election**
J.G. Blumler, A.D. Fox (May 1982, pp.183) £4.50

SEP 7 **Britons in Brussels: Officials in the European Commission and Council Secretariat**
Virginia Willis (January 1983, pp.109) £3.00

SEP 8 **Funding the Arts in Europe**
John Myerscough (October 1984, pp.163) £4.50

SEP 9 **The European Parliament in the EC Policy Process**
A. Robinson, A. Webb (April 1985, pp.59) £2.50

Also, **Regionalism and Supranationalism: Challenges and Alternative to the Nation-State in Canada and Europe** (with the Institute for Research in Public Policy, Canada), (1981, pp.138)   £4.95

The Politics of Agriculture in the European Community
E. Neville-Rolfe (May 1984, pp.547)

Regionalism in European Politics
Roger Morgan (ed.) (April 1986, pp.224)   £15.00

BOOKS

S. Henig (ed.) Political Parties in the European Community, 1979, Allen and Unwin, £16.00

D. Coombes and S.A. Walkland (eds.) Parliaments and Economic Affairs, 1980, Heinemann, £15.50

D. Coombes, Representative Government and Economic Power, 1982, Heinemann, £16.00 (softback £6.95)

R. Morgan and S. Silvestri (eds.) Moderates and Conservatives in Western Europe: Political Parties, The European Community and the Atlantic Alliance (with the Instituto Affari Internazionali, Rome), 1982, Heinemann, £26.00 (Italian edition, 1983)

B. Kohler, Political Forces in Spain, Greece and Portugal, 1982, Butterworths £27.50 (German edition, 1981)

V. Bodganor (ed.) Coalition Government in Western Europe 1982, Heinemann £17.50

V. Bogdanor (ed.) Representatives of the People?, Gower, 1985, £15.00

R. Morgan and C. Bray (eds.) Partners and Rivals in Western Europe: Britain, France and Germany, 1986, Gower, £22.50

NOTTINGHAM UNIVERSITY LIBRARY